"Devonia"

Minehead

SOMERSET

Frome ⊙

Shepton
Mallet

Kings
Weston

Combwich
Bridgewater

Taunton

South Molton

Tiverton

Crediton

Clyst
St Mary

Honiton

DORSET

Weymouth

Exeter

ENGLISH CHANNEL

dbury
Aveton
Gifford

Dartmouth

✗ --- Battles

--- Executions

-- Shipwrecks

GW00671493

A HISTORY OF BIDEFORD

A HISTORY OF BIDEFORD

Duncan Fielder

Phillimore

1985

Published by
PHILLIMORE & CO. LTD.,
Shopwyke Hall, Chichester, Sussex, England

© Duncan Fielder, 1985

ISBN 0 85033 574 4

Printed and bound in Great Britain at
THE CAMELOT PRESS LTD.
Southampton, England

To the people of Torridgeside,
past, present and future,
and my mother, Jane, and Laura

CONTENTS

LIST OF PLATES

(between pages 44 and 45)

LIST OF FIGURES

PREFACE

Researching and writing this history of Bideford has been a deeply moving experience. Metaphorically, I have rubbed shoulders with national figures like the Burrough brothers of Northam, Richard Grenvile of the *Revenge*, and John Hanning Speke, the discoverer of the source of the Nile. I have fought alongside the men of Bideford; I have swopped hangovers with Peter Bagehole, the town drunk; I have sailed in cramped, vomit-fouled emigrant ships. In short, I have been privileged to share the lives of Bidefordians in good times and bad from the dark days of Viking invasions to modern times.

I began this story of Bideford six years ago as a therapeutical exercise after being hit by cardiac troubles. Several times I thought I would never live to finish it. But with the strength and encouragement of my family, I completed what had become a labour of love.

I pray that this history of Bideford does justice to the town and its people.

Bideford
March 1985

DUNCAN FIELDER

ACKNOWLEDGEMENTS

During the six years in which this book has been in preparation, I collected the bulk of the material from the Bideford Public Library. Therefore I would like to express my gratitude to the librarian in charge, Geoff Green, and his staff, for their assistance. I am indebted to the Imperial War Museum for supplying information concerning Private Arthur, V.C. I would like to express my thanks to Devon Library Services, especially Bideford Library, (plates 1, 2, 3, 4, 5, 7, 8, 9, 18, 19, 20, 21, 23, 24, 26) and the National Portrait Gallery, London, (plate 34), for permission to reproduce photographs and portraits, and to Minerva Gallery, Bideford, for help in selecting old pictures of Bideford. I would like to express thanks to James Paterson for supplying me with original pen and ink illustrations and maps at short notice; to Howard Nyman and Paul Bonner for their photographic expertise; to Sheila Muddiman for advice in the preparation of the manuscript; and a big thank you to the many Bidefordians and others who supplied invaluable material.

READING LIST

Alexander & Hooper, *History of Great Torrington*
Ashley, M., *The English Civil War*
Asser, *Life of King Alfred*
Baring-Gould, S., *Devonshire*
Beara, J., *Appledore*
Bideford Gazette
Charlwood, D., *The Long Farewell*
Clowes, W. G., *A History of the Royal Navy*
Cornwall, J., *Revolt of the Peasantry*
Cotton, R. W., *Barnstaple and the Northern Part of Devonshire during the Great Civil War, 1642-1646*
David, R., *Hakluyt's Voyages*
Defoe, D., *A Tour Through the Whole Island of Great Britain*
Devon County Council, *Archaeology of Devon; Coastline of Devon*
Domesday Book, published by Phillimore & Co. Ltd.
Gent, F. J., *The Trial of the Bideford Witches*
Goaman, M., *Old Bideford & District*
Grant, A., *Sailing Ships and Emigrants in Victorian Times*
Greenhill, B., *The Great Emigration*
Greenhill, B. and Gifford, *West Countrymen in Prince Edward Island*
Hole, C., *Witchcraft in England*
Hoskins, W. G., *Devon; Old Devon; Two Thousand Years in Exeter*
Jacob, G., *Looking Back*
Karkeek, P. Q., *Devon Society*
Keeton, G. W., *Lord Chancellor Jeffreys*
Kingsley, C., *Westward Ho!*
Lamplugh, L., *Barnstaple: Town on the Taw*
Larn, R., *Devon Shipwrecks*
Marshall, W., *Rural Economy of the West of England*
Mayo, R., *The Story of Westward Ho!*
Morris, D. R., *The Washing of the Spears*
Mudd, D., *The Cruel Cornish Sea*
North Devon Journal Herald
Oppenheimer, H. M., *Maritime History of Devon*
Owen, C., *The Devon-American Story*

Polwhele, R., *Devon*
Risden, T., *Survey of the County of Devon*
Rogers, Inkerman, *The Bloody Assizes*
Rogers, W. H., *Notes on Bideford*
Rowse, A. L., *Sir Richard Grenvile of the* Revenge
Savage, A., *The Anglo-Saxon Chronicles*
Snell, F. J., *North Devon*
Strong, *Industries of North Devon*
Stuckey, D., *The Bideford, Westward Ho! and Appledore Railway*
Stucley, J., *Sir Bevill Grenvile and His Times*
Thompson, E. P., *The Making of the English Working Class*
Troup, F. Rose, *The Western Rebellion*
Watkins, *A History of Bideford*
White, W., *Devon 1830*
Wigfield, W. MacDonald, *The Monmouth Rebellion: A Social History*
Williams, N. *Sir Francis Drake*
Williamson, H. *Tarka the Otter*
Williamson, J. A., *The English Channel*
Woodham-Smith, C., *The Reason Why*
Worth, R. N., *History of Devon*
Ziegler, P., *The Black Death*

Chapter One

THE EARLY YEARS

SOMETIMES in the depths of winter when Rudyard Kipling's 'stinging, ringing spindrift' lashes over Westward Ho's promenade and Pebble Ridge, a metamorphosis occurs on the seabed when the sea scours aside thousands of tons of sand to reveal the trunks and boles of a petrified forest. Among the stumps can be found the remains of a fossilised midden of a Neolithic village. Compacted into the heap are fish and animal bones together with seeds and flint microliths. Estimated as being between five and seven thousand years old, the midden is among the earliest surviving evidence of man's habitation of the coastline of Bideford Bay. Remains of a substantial Iron Age hill fort are to be found on the northern side of the A39 trunk road at Clovelly Cross, 10 miles to the west of Bideford. Rings of ramparts and dykes encircle an inner area large enough to provide the modern villagers with a football pitch. Other local Iron Age earthworks include Henbury Castle, Buckland Brewer and Berry Castle Camp, Weare Giffard.

About 450 B.C. Carthaginian traders established links with Devon and Cornish silver miners on the Bristol Channel coast. By A.D. 150 the Channel had become an international trade route for Mediterranean nations. Struck by the similarity of the passage between Hartland Point and Lundy Island to that of the seaway between Gibraltar and Africa – the Pillars of Hercules – the Egyptian geographer, Ptolemy, named the Devon feature *Heraclis Promontory* on his map of the known world.

Recent aerial photographs have revealed evidence of a 3.75-acre Roman staging camp at Alverdiscott, on the eastern bank of the Torridge. After A.D. 438 when the last Roman soldier had quit England, Saxon hordes from Northern Europe swarmed into the vacuum. Primarily they came as colonisers and farmers. By the 8th century, the tide of newcomers had washed over the Torridge and lapped the banks of the River Tamar, the boundary between Devon and Cornwall, before coming to a virtual halt. The new arrivals intermarried with the indigenous population, the result being the emergence of an Anglo-Saxon Devon and in A.D. 795 Devon became part of the kingdom of Wessex. For administrative purposes the riverside settlement of Bideford came under the jurisdiction of the Hundred of Shebbear.[1]

Towards the end of Lent of 878 a Viking force, which had invaded the North Devon-Somerset coast of King Alfred's kingdom of Wessex, was destroyed at 'Arx Cynuit' by local militia. To illustrate the historical background and the significance of the Saxon victory, the contemporaneous entry in the *Anglo-Saxon Chronicle* describes the battle and its aftermath:

1

The [Viking] stole in midwinter, after Twelfthnight, to Chippenham. They rode to Wessex and occupied it, and drove many of the people over the sea; the other, greater part they overcame, except King Alfred with a little company, which with difficulty went through the woods onto inaccessible moors. The same winter Iwar's brother Healfdene [sons of Ragnar Leatherbreechs] was in Wessex, in Devon, with 23 ships: he was killed there and 800 men with him and 40 men of his retinue. There the standard was taken, which they call the Raven. At Easter, King Alfred, with a little company, built a fort at Athelney, and from the fort kept fighting the force, with the help of those at Somerset who were nearest. In the seventh week after Easter he rode to Ecbryth's Stone, east of Selwood. All those of Somerset came to meet him, and those of Wiltshire and Hampshire, the part this side of the sea; they were glad of his coming. After one night, he went from the camp of Iley Oak, and after a night at Edington, and there fought with the whole force and put them to flight. He rode after them to the fort and besieged it for fourteen days and nights. Then the force gave him hostages, and great oaths that they would go from his kingdom; they also promised that their king would receive baptism.

Asser, Bishop of Sherborne, Alfred's friend and biographer, adds further details of the battle in his *Life of King Alfred*. While he does not name the Viking commander, he implies that he was Ubbi, or Hubba, elder son of Ragnar, and not Halfdeane as stated in the *Anglo-Saxon Chronicle*:

In the same year the brother of Ivar and Halfdeane sailed with twenty-three ships from Pembroke [where he had spent the winter], after slaughtering many of the Christians there, and came to Devon there, acting on an erroneous assumption, he met an unhappy death with 1,200 men, at the hands of the king's thegns and in front of the stronghold at Cynuit. For many of the king's thegns, with their followers, had shut themselves up for safety inside the stronghold; and when the Vikings saw the stronghold was unprepared and altogether unfortified (except for ramparts thrown up in our fashion), they made no attempt to storm it, since by the lie of the land that place is very secure from every direction except at the east, as I myself have seen. Instead they began to besiege it, thinking that those men would soon give way, forced by hunger, thirst and the siege, since there is no water near the stronghold. But it did not turn out as they thought. For the Christians, long before they were liable to suffer want in any way, were divinely inspired and judging it much better to gain either death or victory, burst out unexpectedly at dawn against the Vikings and, by virtue of their aggressiveness, from the very outset they overwhelmed the enemy in large part, together with their King, a few escaping by flight to the ships.

Where did the lost battle of Arx Cynuit take place? Northam historian, R.S. Vidal, believed in 1804 that Hubba and his Vikings stormed ashore at Appledore Skern[2] and advanced inland to lay siege to Kenwith Castle defended by Odun, Earl of Devon and his men, and that Kenwith was indeed Arx Cynuit. He argued that the name must be a derivation of 'Cynuit', while a vanished stone on the Torridge shoreline at Appledore called the Whibblestone had to be the place where Hubba was buried because 'It is so similar in sound [to Hubba] that the most scrupulous entymologist could ask no better after 1,000 years'.

He claimed that a bend in the Northam-Appledore road, where Viking artefacts were alleged to have been unearthed by roadmen, traditionally known as Bloody Corner, was the place where Hubba and his jarls were slaughtered:

Thus we have a tradition which can be traced from the reign of Queen Elizabeth I to today, placing the site of the original attack at Kenwith and the fiercest stand of the disastrous retreat at Bloody Corner, Northam.

Eighty-six years later, Charles Chappell, antiquarian and supporter of the Vidal theory, had a memorial erected at Bloody Corner commemorating Hubba's death and the Anglo-Saxon victory. The inscription reads:

Stop, stranger, stop,   Who was slain by
Near this spot lies buried   King Alfred the Great
King Hubba the Dane   In a bloody retreat.

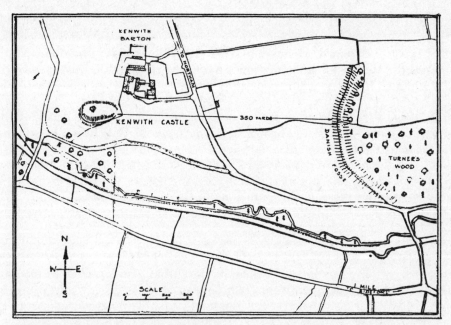

Fig. 1. Kenwith Castle, Northam. This was possibly the site of the lost battle of Arx Cynuit, A.D. 878, where Ubba the Dane was slain and his Viking army destroyed.

Modern historians favour earthworks at Countisbury, Somerset, to be the likely site of Arx Cynuit. Another contender for the battle is Combwich on the River Parrett, near Bridgwater in Somerset's Isle of Athelney.

Name association alone, whether it has its origins in Countisbury, Combwich or Kenwith, cannot be taken as proof of the battle's location. Until the riddle is solved by irrefutable historical evidence, Kenwith must remain as a contender for the site of the lost battle of Arx Cynuit, an English victory which did so much to dispel the myth of Viking invincibility.

However, the Vikings were redoubtable foes and they continued to make sporadic attacks on the North Devon coast. From time to time they occupied Lundy Island[3] in order to launch raids on Devon. In 988, the English thegn, Goda, and many of his men were killed in one of these punitive incursions. Nine years after Goda's death, the Norsemen sailed from the River Severn, ravaging and slaughtering coastal communities of Somerset, Devon and Cornwall before rounding Land's End to land at the River Tamar. There they marched inland laying waste to the countryside, burning Lydford, and sacking Tavistock Monastery.

On 14 October 1066, William, Duke of Normandy, landed in Sussex to claim England's disputed crown. As darkness fell over Senlac Hill, Hastings, the corpse of Harold, the last of the Saxon monarchs, lay among the bodies of his followers. William followed up his crushing victory with customary ruthlessness. Having seized Dover, he advanced on London where he was crowned King of England in Westminster Abbey on Christmas Day.

His wife, Queen Mathilda, claimed direct descent from Alfred the Great. Since early girlhood she had borne an unreciprocated passion for Brihtric the Fair, an English nobleman and wealthy landowner who, as a young man, had served as English

Ambassador at the court of her father, the Count of Flanders. After completing his tour of duty at the Flanders court, Brihtric returned to his estates in England which included that of the Manor of Bideford. Meanwhile, William of Normandy, smitten by Mathilda's beauty, asked the Count for his daughter's hand in marriage. Receiving a favourable answer, he pursued her in a stormy courtship lasting several years before their marriage in 1053.

Mathilda never forgave Brihtric for his indifference and when she became Queen of England, she ordered his arrest. Thrown into a dungeon at Winchester Castle, Brihtric died in suspicious circumstances.

Acceptance of the Norman dynasty had become established in North Devon by 1069, so much so that, during the summer of that year, men of the Torridge estuary fought a rebel army led by the three illegitimate sons of the dead King Harold:

> After this Harold's sons from Ireland at midsummer with 64 ships came into the mouth of the Taw, and went unexpectedly inland.
>
> Earl Brian came upon them unawares with no small host, fought them, and killed all the best men in that fleet; the other small host fled out to the ships, and Harold's sons went back to Ireland.

William proved to be not only a ruthless monarch but also a rapacious tax gatherer. Four years after Mathilda's death, in 1086, a year of great famine and pestilence, he commanded that a nationwide survey of England's taxable potential be made. His tax commissioners held inquests of such exactitude that the *Anglo-Saxon Chronicle* moaned that:

> So very closely did the King cause the survey to be made that there was not one single hide nor rod of land, nor further it is shameful to tell though it seemed to him no shame to do it, not an ox, a cow, a pig, was left out, that was not set in his document.

Compiled into two bulky volumes, the laboriously written returns were dubbed the 'Domesday Book', as no appeal was allowed against the assessments.

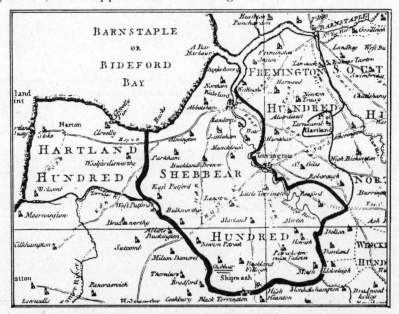

Fig. 2.   Shebbear Hundred, from Domesday Book: Devon, 1086.
'A grove from which spear shafts can be cut.'

The entry for Bideford is as follows:

BIDEFORD. Before 1066 it paid tax for 3 hides. Land for 26 ploughs. In lordship 4 ploughs; 14 slaves; ½ hide.
30 villagers and 8 smallholders with 20 ploughs and 2½ hides. Meadow, 10 acres; pasture, 20 acres; woodland, 150 acres.
18 cattle; 300 sheep.
It pays £16.
A fishery was attached to this manor before 1066; it pays 25s.[4]

On Brihtric's death, the Manor of Bideford reverted to the Crown. William then bestowed the title on his cousin, Richard Grandivala. Later the name became anglicised as Grenvile.[5] The Grenvile family were to remain lords of Bideford Manor for nearly seven centuries. William gave Brihtric's Manor of Northam to the Abbot of Caen. Domesday Book records the Manor thus:

Land of St. Stephen's of Caen
St. Stephen's Church, Caen holds NORTHAM from the King.
Brictric held it before 1066. It paid tax for 2 hides and ½ virgate of land. Land for 20 ploughs. In lordship 3 ploughs; 8 slaves; 1 virgate.
23 villagers and 5 smallholders with 14 ploughs and 1½ hides and ½ virgate. 1 pigman.
2 salt-houses which pay 10s; a fishery which pays 30d; meadow, 15 acres; woodland, 24 acres; underwood, 30 acres; pasture, 15 acres. 23 cattle; 340 sheep; 5 [goats?].
Value formerly and now £12.

The salt-houses consisted of shallow pools in which tidal water was trapped. Allowed to evaporate, the resultant salt crystals were collected to provide essential salt for preserving meat and fish as well as for culinary usage.

Those who lived within the boundaries of the Manor of Northam secured the 'potwalloping' rights to free grazing of livestock on Northam Burrows. To qualify as a potwalloper, people were supposed to have set up cooking pots in the Manor bounds for not less than six months. The ancient practice whereby potwallopers gathered at the Pebbleridge on Whit Mondays to throw back stones dislodged by winter gales ceased many years ago. Nowadays the job is done by bulldozers.

The Domesday entry for Appledore is as follows:

Ralph of Bruyère also holds APPLEDORE from Baldwin. Leofnoth held it before 1066. It paid tax for 1 virgate of land. Land for 1½ ploughs; as many there, with 1 slave and 2 villagers and 1 smallholder.
Meadow, 2 acres. 3 cattle; 25 sheep.
Formerly 5s; value now 10s.

It will be noted that in Appledore's case, the taxmen doubled its rental value.

The origins of the place-names of the communities of Shebbear Hundred on the tidal reaches of the Torridge can be summarised thus – River Torridge, the rough river; Bideford/East-the-Water, a fording place on a river, or perhaps Bieda's of Bidna's Ford; Northam, northern meadow; Appledore, a place where apple trees grow, alternatively from the Celtic *Pwll Dwr*, a deep pool of water.

By the latter half of the 13th century, the need to supplement the dangerous ford upstream of Bideford by bridging the Torridge had become critical. 'Sir' Richard Gurnay, or Gornay, Bideford's parish priest, must take the credit for being the driving force behind the building of the town's first bridge.[6] The work began sometime between 1280 and 1291. Despite help and encouragement from the Grenvile family, the cost of construction proved to be beyond Bideford's resources. Gurnay turned to his superior,

Peter Quivel, Bishop of Exeter, for help. Impressed by Gurnay's appeal, Quivel granted him a licence to sell indulgences to finance the building of the bridge and subsequent maintenance costs.

Gurnay's 677ft.-long wooden bridge with its 24 spans of differing lengths was a major achievement of medieval civil engineering. At each end of the bridge, Gurnay built chapels for the sale of indulgences; at East-the-Water, All Saints, and at the west end, Allhallows. The roadway was barely wide enough to accommodate pack animals and pedestrians at the same time and heavier transport still had to face the dangers of the ford crossing. A trust comprised of 24 elected trustees or feoffs administered the bridge. As the bridge aged, so deterioration of the fabric set in. Time and again the feoffs had to find the money to carry out urgent repairs. Successive Exeter bishops renewed Gurnay's original licence to sell indulgences but in 1460 the feoffs judged the bridge to be on the verge of collapse after 170 years of continuous usage.

The architect of the new longbridge adopted an ingenious technique of construction. Instead of demolishing the wooden framework, his masons encased the sound oaken beams in a jacket of stone. The new bridge therefore bore a close resemblance to Gurnay's original structure incorporating, however, an important innovation. Massive cuttwaters were tied into bedrock to carry the weight of the Gothic arches which reflected the religious influence of its design. Although the roadway remained narrow, niches were built out of the parapets to provide pedestrians with shelter from traffic.

On the western bank of the Torridge stands Bideford's parish church of St Mary. Originally built by Saxons with mud and wattle, but with a stone tower, it was replaced in c.1259 by a much larger church, built about the old one, so that devotions would not be interrupted. The Norman font is unusual, being circular when the majority of surviving examples are square. The Grenvile family held the patronage of St Mary's more or less continuously until 1727.

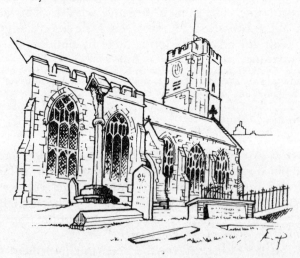

Fig. 3. St Mary's church. Bideford's parish church,
parts of which date back to Norman times.

Through Sir Richard Grenvile's influence at the Court of Henry III, Bideford became a Borough in 1217. In the last year of Henry's reign, a later Sir Richard Grenvile obtained a Royal Charter for the town. A town seal was granted together with the right for the town to hold a market every Monday, and an annual fair on the Feast Day of St Margaret the Virgin. Common law forbade the holding of a market within six miles of the established town market.

Despite the growing importance of its fishing, woollen and shipbuilding industries, Bideford remained in the shadow of its more prosperous neighbour, Barnstaple, and it was not until the French and Scottish wars of the 14th century that the town and Torridgeside came into their own. Between 1308 and 1322, successive monarchs made demands on west-country ports to supply shipping to ferry armies to war. Tawmouth (Appledore) contributed seven ships and 120 men to Edward III's French campaign, culminating in the English victory at the Battle of Crécy in 1346. Edward had prepared well for the campaign. To form a nucleus of trained bowmen, he ordered all able-bodied men to practise with longbows at archery butts. To encourage them, he banned the playing of handball, football or hockey, coursing, cockfighting or other such idle pastimes, on pain of death. Bideford's butts were situated in what is now Buttgarden Street. Advanced archery training took place in Wooda, on the southern side of Torridge Hill.

While the Crécy battle was being fought, the Black Death raged through France and the rest of Europe. By August 1348, the pestilence had spread across the English Channel and struck the Dorset port of Melcombe Regis (Weymouth). From thence it extended throughout the west country. At the church-less parish of Templeton, between South Molton and Tiverton, corpses of plague victims were taken by the cartload for burial in consecrated ground at Witheridge. At Hartland, the Abbot of the Priory perished. No record exists of Bideford's mortality rate. By 1349 the plague had spent itself in Devon, leaving an estimated third of the population dead and the feudal infrastructure in ruins. But despite these ravages, foreign wars continued and correspondingly heavier taxes had to be raised from the survivors. Bideford did not escape:

> John Toky, the collector in the ports of Barnstaple, Towmouth, Ilfridecombe [Ilfracombe] and Dunsterre [Dunster] are directed that the following subsidy on all imports shall be levied for one year, to wit 2s. on every sack of wool, 2s. on every wool fell, 4s. on every last of hides, and a gold crown or 40d. on every tun of wine, 6d. on every other merchandise as well herring and fish as other wares for the sustenance and arming of such ships which are employed in convoying and defence duties.

Tax demands to underwrite foreign wars of little or no concern to West Country people were fairly constant during the next hundred years and inflamed resentment against the Crown. In 1497, the parishioners of St Keverne in Cornwall's Lizard peninsula revolted against both penal taxation and the excesses of a corrupt clergy. Led by Myghal an Gof, the village blacksmith, and Thomas Flamanck, a lawyer, a band of Cornishmen set out for London to seek redress for their grievances from Henry VII. After crossing the Torridge at Bideford, Myghal paused at Horwood to nail a lucky horseshoe on the door of St Michael's church. But good fortune did not favour the Cornishmen. Henry refused to listen to the pleas of 'lewd peasants' and instead he loosed his army on them at Blackheath Common. Both Myghal and Flamanck were captured and executed at Tower Hill. As to the fate of other prisoners who escaped the gallows, many were sold into slavery at 1s.0d. each.

The year 1546 dawned with England yet again at war with the old enemy France. Henry VIII ordered Devon to muster 500 men for war service. Sir Richard Grenvile,

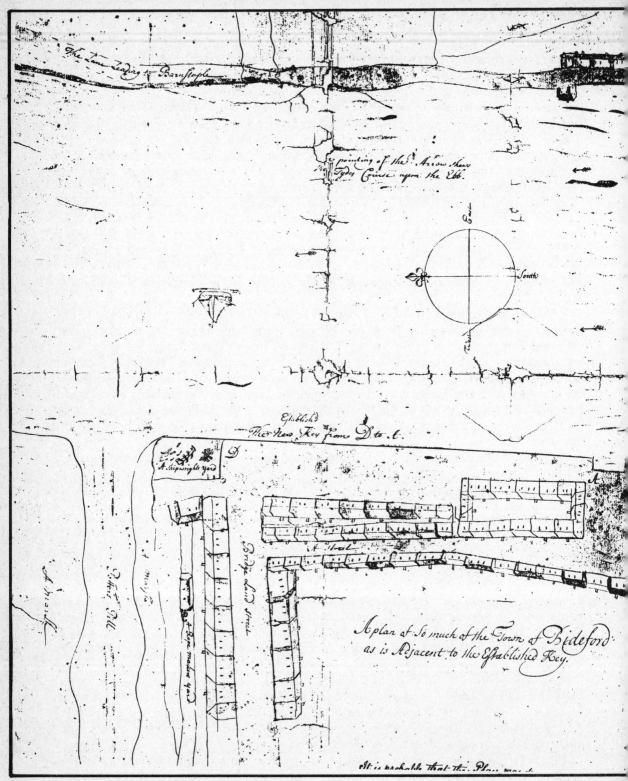

Fig. 4 Probably the oldest surviving map of Bideford (*c.* 1690) showing Nathaniel Gascoyne's development of Bridgeland Street's Quay.

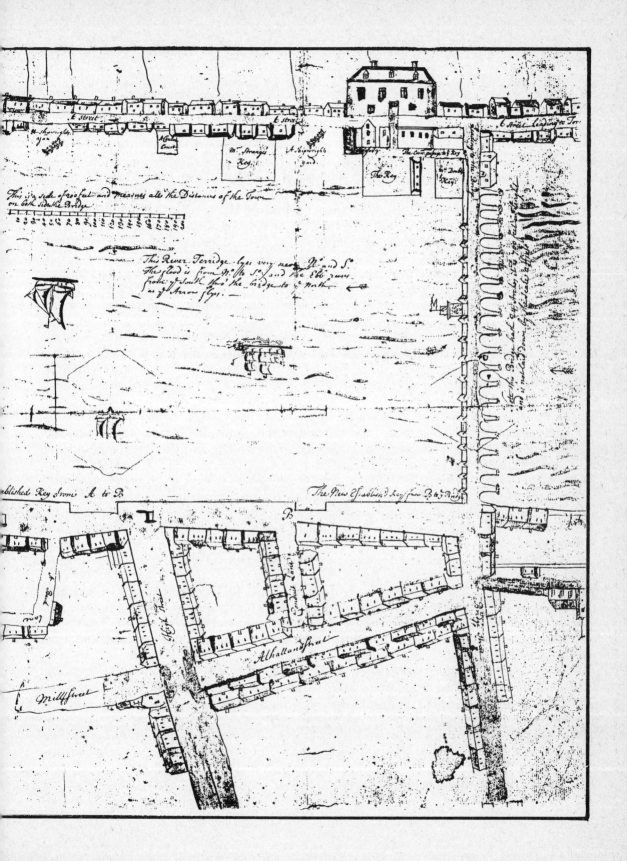

of Bideford and Stow, Kilkhampton, England's last governor of Calais, and father of Roger, led the North Devon contingent to Dover for embarkation for France.

In their turn, the French planned to invade England. In July, Admiral d'Annebault, commanding a fleet of 225 sail and 30,000 men, a force far larger than that of the Spanish Armada 40 years later, sailed to capture Portsmouth. On 19 July, the French dropped anchor off the Isle of Wight. King Henry took personal command of Portsmouth's defences. In the harbour, Admiral of the Fleet, Lord Lisle waited with 100 ships and 12,000 men for a favourable wind to engage the enemy. Lisle's flagship was the massive *Henry Grace à Dieu*, 1,000 tons, the pride of Henry's navy. His Vice-Admiral, Sir George Carew, flew his standard from the masthead of the carrack *Mary Rose*, 800 tons,[7] 'the flower of all ships that ever sailed'. Sir Richard Grenvile's son, Roger, captained the great ship.

The 19 July was a hot and windless day. Henry dined aboard the flagship with his senior officers. During the meal, lookouts warned that enemy-oared galleys were fast approaching so the King returned to Southsea Castle. The becalmed *Henry Grace à Dieu* became the main target of the French. In the afternoon, a breeze sprang up, billowing out the sails of the *Mary Rose*. With her decks cleared for action, and her cannon run out, the massive galleon layed into wind to give support to the flagship. Suddenly her open gunports dipped below the waves. Seawater rushed in and the ship immediately took on a fatal list.

From the battlements of Southsea Castle, Henry and his entourage watched in horror as the *Mary Rose* capsized. Sinking like a stone, she took over 700 men to their deaths. Only 30 survived the tragedy; Sir Roger Grenvile and Sir George Carew were not among them. Old Sir Richard took Roger's young widow and her three-year-old son, Richard, under his wing.

Related by marriage, the Grenvile and Carew families were to be caught up in the tragedy of Devon's Prayer Book War of 1549. Reminders of the Prayer Book War are to be found among the treasures of St Mary's church, Bideford, and St Margaret's, Northam. The former possesses a chained Protestant English Bible made compulsory by Edward VI's Act of Uniformity of 1549, a consolidation of his father's Reformation. St Margaret's treasures include fragments of the Kyries, a form of sung Catholic Latin liturgy outlawed by the same Act.

Bideford had not escaped from Protestant vandalism following Henry's break with Rome. St Mary's Norman font was purloined by a bigot who used it as a pigs' trough. It was eventually recovered and returned to the church none the worse for wear. Elsewhere, religious houses at Frithelstock and Barnstaple were sacked and their inmates dispersed.

For ordinary people, 1549 proved to be a disastrous year. Weeks of wet weather in the spring had caused crop failure while cattle murrain decimated livestock. A debased currency led to a rapid rise in inflation resulting in a doubling in the price of corn in two years. Many peasants had good reason to hate the gentry for their arrogance and the clergy for their corruption, while the seizure of commonland by grasping landowners drove the dispossessed to revolt. For Devonians, the prime cause of their rebellion was religious. From Whit Sunday, 1549, the wearing of Catholic vestments by clergy, the usage of Latin liturgy, and all symbols of Catholicism were forbidden. Church services in English preached from Archbishop Cranmer's Book of Common Prayer became compulsory, as did Martin Coverdale's English Bible.

The radical and arbitrary changes struck at the very roots of the predominantly Catholic beliefs of Devon's peasantry. A prayer in the new litany did little to make the Protestant form of worship more acceptable to them:

From all seditions and privy conspiracies from the tyrant of the Bishop of Rome and all his detestable enormities, Good Lord deliver us.

To aggravate an already potentially explosive situation the Act of Uniformity had been promulgated by a sickly 12-year-old boy king. A fanatical Protestant himself, Edward ruled through a Protectorate headed by his uncle, Edward Seymour, Duke of Somerset, who had enriched himself by sequestering church land.

Sampford Courtenay, a picturesque and remote village a few miles north-east of Okehampton, was to be the unlikely venue for the outbreak of the Prayer Book War. On Whit Sunday at matins, 70-year-old Father William Harper, who owed his living to Katherine Parr, Henry VIII's widow, appeared before his congregation in St Andrew's church attired in plain robes to conform with the Act, and not the elaborate Catholic vestments he had worn hitherto. Then he conducted the liturgy from Cranmer's Prayer Book. At the end of the devotions, the villagers scornfully dismissed the service as nothing but a 'Christmas game'. Their spokesmen, Thomas Underhill, tailor, and William Segar, labourer, desired of Harper what form of service he proposed to conduct on Whit Monday, a church's ale holiday when beer flowed freely. Harper answered that he had no alternative but to comply with the law. Underhill retorted that the villagers demanded an immediate return to Henry VIII's Catholic form of prayer until Edward VI reached the age of 24, according to their interpretation of Henry's will. In the face of the villagers' hostility, Harper relented. On that ill-fated spring morning, Harper came before his flock, 'revesseth himself in his old Popish attire and sayeth mass and all such services as in times past accustomed', much to the delight and satisfaction of his congregation.

News of the extraordinary events in a hitherto peaceful village soon came to the notice of Sir Hugh Pollard, the King's Justice, of Kings Nympton:

being advertised how disorderly and contrary to the laws had been done in the Church . . . and how the common people were clustered and assembled together to continue and maintain their lewd and disordered behaviour . . .

With alarming news of a Cornish uprising led by a dissident minor aristocrat, Lord Arundel, Pollard had to act swiftly to defuse the situation before Devon was engulfed by civil war.

Whilst their grievances bore similarities to those of the peasants of Sampford Courtenay, the Cornishmen's resentment had been further exacerbated by the savagery with which the Crown had suppressed an insurrection at St Keverne, the volatile village of the martyred hero, Myghol an Gof. Now a week before the events in Sampford Courtenay, Arundel's Cornishmen, including the brothers John and William Winslade, landowners of Buckland Brewer, had crossed the Tamar, captured Plymouth, and were approaching Crediton. During their advance, the rebels had arrested old Sir Richard Grenvile and his family who had taken refuge in Trematon Castle, Saltash. In the light of subsequent atrocities committed by the King's men against captured rebels, Sir Richard and his ladies, although roughly handled, were treated with commendable leniency by their captors.

When Sir Hugh Pollard and his colleagues arrived at Sampford Courtenay, they found the main street barricaded, and the villagers loth to parley with them. Although

Pollard had sufficient retainers to rush the roadblocks and end the trouble by force, he tried to reason with the excited peasants. This hope was dashed by the appearance in the village of William Hellyon, a local magnate who decided he could bring the peasants to heel by a mixture of bluster and threats. Instead, his overbearing attitude inflamed the situation. Seizing him, the angry villagers frogmarched him to their headquarters in the Church House. Even in the face of intense hostility, Hellyon had not the wit to bridle his tongue:

> He so earnestly reproved them for their rebellion and so sharply threatened them of an evil success, that they fell in a rage with him; and not only with evil words reviled him, but also as he was going out of the Church House, and going down the stairs, one of them, Lethbridge, with a bill hook struck him in the neck, and immediately notwithstanding his piteful requests and lamentations, a number of the rest fell upon him and cut him in small pieces.

The first blood of the Prayer Book War had been spilt. Father Harper ordered Hellyon's remains to be buried. Instead of being laid to rest in a grave dug east to west, the villagers interred the mutilated corpse in a grave dug north to south to signify that Hellyon had died a heretic. Aware that they could expect no mercy from the King for murdering a royal officer, the villagers gathered weapons and marched off to join the Cornish rebels at Crediton, 15 miles away.

The dramatic news of the Sampford Courtenay uprising spread

> as a cloud with a violent wind and as a thunderclap sounding through the whole country and all the common people so well allowed and like thereof that they clapped their hands for joy and argued in one mind to have the same in every of their several parishes.

From all over the county, particularly from the north-west, sympathisers converged on Crediton to support the men of Sampford Courtenay. Henry Lee, mayor of Torrington, headed a contingent of townspeople. Lord Arundel's secretary, John Coffin, led a group from Alwington,[8] North Devon. The morale of the Devon rebels was high and above the vanguard of their crusading army floated the banner of the Five Wounds of Christ.

It took nearly three weeks for Lord Protector Somerset to appreciate the gravity of the Western rebellion. He appointed John Russell, Duke of Bedford and Lord Privy Seal, to be President of the Council of the West, thereby making him military overlord for the Western Peninsula. As well, Somerset despatched Sir Peter Carew and his uncle Sir Gawan to deliver an ultimatum to the rebels which ordered them either to lay down their arms immediately, surrender Hellyon's killers and disperse peaceably, or face the full wrath of the law.

When Sir Peter attempted to deliver the document to rebels manning a roadblock on the outskirts of Crediton, he was shouted down. Sir Peter 'accustomed to cross swords with French cavalry, was not to be daunted by village churls'. Without bothering to reconnoitre the rebels' defences, he led a charge against the road block. Meeting well-organised resistance and suffering a number of casualties, he withdrew. During the confused fighting that followed, thatched barns on both sides of the road burst into flames. The rebel defenders fled. The rout spread to the rebels in Crediton and when Carew entered the town he found it deserted except for the sick and the elderly.

The rebels quickly regained their confidence. Proud of the manner they had faced up to Carew's retainers, they adopted 'The Battle of the Barns' as a rallying cry. Men and women flocked to join their crusade, and peasants fortified their villages against royalist attacks. The Devon and Cornishmen organised themselves into four divisions under the overall command of Lord Arundel. John Coffin served as second-in-command to fellow

Devonian, Henry Bury. Having drawn up a humble petition listing their grievances – the Sixteen Articles – the rebel high command despatched the document to the Lord Protector in London. Not surprisingly, the Protectorate dismissed it as the work of lewd and 'light' peasantry. Meanwhile truce negotiations between the villagers of Clyst St Mary and Carew's emissaries had proved abortive. The peasants might have accepted the royalist terms if they had known the Protector had sent a mercenary army consisting of Italian arquebusiers, German infantry and Burgundian cavalry, originally earmarked for an invasion of Scotland, to Lord Russell's camp at Honiton. Against these battle-hardened continental veterans, Arundel's rustic army stood little or no chance.

After the fighting at Crediton, the rebels advanced on Exeter. If Arundel had hoped the Exonians would join the rebel cause, he was grievously mistaken. He found that Mayor John Blackaller had locked the town gates and defended the walls against him. Deprived of recruits, weaponry and gunpowder, Arundel had to split his already inadequate forces, leaving behind precious manpower to protect his lines of communication by laying siege to the town. With his main force he advanced westwards to take positions on the banks of the River Otter. Here sympathisers from Somerset swelled the rebel ranks, bringing up their strength to about eight thousand.

Towards the end of July, Russell struck camp at Honiton and marched on Fenny Bridges to seize the crossings over the Otter. After a hard fought battle, in which Sir Gawan Carew received an arrow wound in the arm, the royalists seized the bridges, killing 300 of the rebels for the loss of less than one hundred.

Falling back on Clyst St Mary, the rebels turned the riverside village into a fortress. But, after fierce hand-to-hand fighting, the rebels' resistance was crushed and the river crossings secured.

The capture of Clyst St Mary opened the road to Exeter. Sweeping aside desperate resistance, the royalists reached Woodbury Common. Here royalist scouts reported the approach of a rebel column. To have the maximum number of men to meet the threatened attack, the royalist commander, Lord Grey, ordered the slaughter of prisoners of war so that their guards could be released for fighting duties. But the report was false and 200 were slaughtered needlessly.

On 6 August, the royalist army arrived at Exeter's south gate. The next morning Russell entered the starving city ending the six week siege. Now came the time for retribution. Ably assisted by the King's Provost Marshal, Sir Anthony Kingston, Russell began the systematic execution of rebels and their sympathisers, caught both inside and outside the city walls. After nine days of blood-letting, Russell, at the head of an army of 8,000, marched out of Exeter to crush rebel survivors who had retreated to Sampford Courtenay to make a last stand. Among the commanders were John Coffin, John Bury, the Winslade brothers and Thomas Underhill.

To the north of the village, Russell's mercenaries rushed Arundel's frontline, killing between 500 and 600 rebels including Underhill. In a pincer movement supported by artillery, the royalists overran the rebels' main camp, slaughtering a further 500 rebels. In the pursuit of fugitives, another 700 died.

To all intents and purposes, the tragedy of the Prayer Book War was over, crushed in the smoking rubble of the village where it had begun three months previously. But a handful of rebels had escaped the holocaust of Sampford Courtenay. Arundel and William Winslade fled to Launceston where they eventually surrendered to old Sir Richard Grenvile who had been imprisoned in the castle. John Coffin and John Bury led a band of escapers northwards up the Exe valley. Near Tiverton, royalist pursuers caught up with them and many of those captured were executed immediately. John Coffin evaded capture and, with other survivors, struck eastwards into friendly Somerset. Between Somerton and Bruton, at King's Weston, Sir Peter Carew cornered his quarry. For the rebels there was to be no escape. Exhausted by forced marches, verging on starvation and short of ammunition, they fought for their lives against a vastly superior enemy. After 'great slaughter and execution' the survivors were forced to surrender. John Coffin and John Bury were among the hundrd or so prisoners taken. Many of the ordinary prisoners were executed on the spot. Others were taken to Bath, Frome, Shepton Mallet and other West Country towns for execution to remind the peasantry of the consequences of rebellion against the Crown. Gentlemen, including Coffin, Bury and the Winslades joined Arundel at Exeter prison before being taken to London for a show trial. Arundel and Bury were hanged, drawn and quartered at Tyburn Pike.

The fate of John Coffin is unknown. He may have been pardoned, or died either from wounds or prison fever. Of the fate of other leading characters involved in the Prayer Book War, the Lord Protector fell from favour and was executed in 1552. In the following year, the boy king, Edward VI, died. Henry Lee, mayor of Torrington, perished in the fighting; Lord Russell, who enriched himself by grabbing sequestered Devon church land including that of Tavistock, died in his bed. Father Harper of Sampford Courtenay remained vicar of the village until his resignation in 1558.

No cenotaph commemorates the thousands of West Country people who died in the Prayer Book War. With them died their Catholic beliefs. Before the century was out, their sons and daughters had embraced the new Protestantism with the same dedication their forebears had embraced the old religion.

Concomitant with the Prayer Book War was an incident in St Mary's churchyard, the effect of which led to changes in the law. During his incumbency of St Mary's, the Reverend Richard Gilbert fell foul of Sir William Coffin of Portledge. While riding by the church, Sir William's attention was drawn to a heated altercation between Gilbert and a funeral cortège, who had brought the coffin of a poor peasant to the cemetery for burial. The mourners explained to Coffin that the vicar had refused to conduct the service until he received the deceased's best cow as payment of his fee.

Sir William ordered Gilbert to conduct the service immediately. When he refused, Coffin told the mourners to bury the priest alive in the newly dug grave. The mourners needed no further encouragement. Seizing Gilbert they bundled him into the hole, and set to with their shovels. When only his head was visible above the soil did the mourners pay heed to the wretched man's shrieks for mercy and his promise that he would bury the old man without taking his fee.

The Bishop of Exeter brought the incident before Parliament where Sir William argued his reasons for his actions so convincingly that Parliament enacted a Mortuary Act to go on the Statute book. The law established a standardised scale of burial fees and made it compulsory for priests to be responsible for the burial of the dead.

Chapter Two

ELIZABETHAN SEA DOGS (1555-1590)

WHILST THE DRAMA of the Prayer Book War was being acted out in South Devon, Stephen Burrough, of Burrough House, Bone Hill, Northam, assimilated the hard lessons of practical navigation and seamanship on the fickle waters of the Torridge estuary and Bideford Bay. By 1555, his skills had come to the attention of the veteran explorer, Sebastian Cabot of the Muscovy Company, who selected the 24-year-old to navigate a flotilla bound for northern seas to discover an Arctic Sea route to the Pacific Ocean and China, thereby opening up a spice and silk route to replace that of the Eastern Mediterranean, cut off from Europe by Moslem expansionism.

On 20 May 1553 when the boy King Edward VI lay dying at his riverside palace of Greenwich, the flotilla sailed down the Thames on the first leg of its momentous journey. Sir Hugh Willoughby commanded the expedition from his flagship, *Bona Speranza* (120 tons). Stephen Burrough sailed aboard the *Edward Bonaventura* as second-in-command to Richard Chancellor. The 90-ton *Bona Confidanta* made up the fleet.

Towards the end of the month, the ships made landfall at Norway's Lofoten Islands. After revictualling, Willoughby headed for the Barents Sea. Having rounded the North Cape, which Stephen Burrough named, the flotilla ran into foul weather and was dispersed. After waiting in vain for a week at a prearranged station for the other ships to join him, Chancellor hauled up his anchor and sailed on alone into the uncharted wastes of the Arctic Ocean. With winter approaching and the sea rapidly freezing solid, Willoughby was forced to turn back to seek shelter. Stephen Burrough navigated the *Bonaventura* to a safe, ice-free anchorage at Kholmorgoi, a Russian settlement on the White Sea, close to the modern port of Archangel. From there, the Englishmen began the 1,000 mile journey to Moscow.

After enduring incredible hardships, Chancellor and his men reached Tsar Ivan the Terrible's primitive capital city. Here Chancellor concluded diplomatic and trading agreements with the Russian monarch. Although Chancellor's expedition had not discovered the elusive north-eastern passage to the riches of the east, the skill of a Northam seaman had been instrumental in dragging the Russian bear out of its forest wilderness and into the mainstream of world politics. For better or for worse, the world would never be the same again.

Two years later, on 25 April 1556, Stephen Burrough left Gravesend in the diminutive 22-ton pinnace *Searchthrift*, convoying two merchantmen to North Russia. Included in his crew of nine was his younger brother, William. Parting company with the convoy off the entrance to the White Sea, Stephen steered a course eastwards in another bid to find the North-East Passage. On 1 August he landed on the south-west coast of Novaya Zemlya Island and explored and charted the strait between that island and Waigatsch Island, which he called the Burrough Straits. Overwintering at Kholmorgoi, he returned to England in the spring of the following year.

Dissatisfied with the low professional standards of English seamanship, Stephen obtained permission to have Martin Cortes' handbook on navigation *Arte de Navigar* translated into English. It revolutionised the expertise of English shipmasters, enabling them to compete on level terms with their continental rivals. Stephen's epic voyages caught the imagination of Spanish naval authorities and in 1560, he was invited to Sevile where his hosts showered him with honours and gifts, including a pair of scented gloves 'worth five or six ducats'.

Stephen returned to Russia for the last time in 1561. Two years later Queen Elizabeth appointed him to be Chief Pilot of the Medway and a Master of the Navy in recognition of his exploits. He died at the age of 60, and was buried with full naval honours at Chatham.

After his adventures with his brother Stephen in the *Searchthrift*, William Burrough continued to serve the Muscovy Company. In 1570, he commanded a flotilla hunting down pirates in the Baltic Sea. These included renegade Englishmen, who preyed on Muscovy Company's merchantmen plying between England and newly opened Russian Baltic seaports. His mission met with success:

> The said William Burrough and his company had discomfited and taken to the number of ten sail (whereof three were prizes) and ten of the chief pirates were hanged at Wapping; one of them, named Thomas Walton, as he went towards the gallows rent his venetian breeches of crimson taffeta and distributed the same to some of his old acquaintances as stood about him.

In 1587, Elizabeth, alarmed at reports of a Spanish invasion Armada gathering at Cadiz, ordered Sir Francis Drake to make a punitive strike against the harbour to disrupt the Spanish preparations. Drake chose William Burrough to be his second-in-command. There was little rapport between the impulsive, audacious Drake and the cautious and professional William. On 2 April, Drake's strike force set sail for Cadiz. Drake flew his standard on the *Elizabeth Bonaventura*, 600 tons, 47 cannon, while William Burrough commanded the *Golden Lion*, 500 tons, 38 cannon.

Even before the start of the raid on 12 April differences over tactics had soured the relationship between the two men. As the raid progressed so did their disagreements. Drake interpreted Burrough's caution as cowardice while Burrough accused his chief of dangerous recklessness. At the end of the raid, which had set back the Armada's sailing by a year, Drake had Burrough clapped in irons and shipped back to England to stand trial. Drake sailed south to sack Sagres. Meanwhile Burrough, released by his jailers, had arrived back in England in time to plead his case to the Queen before Drake's arrival. Her Tudor temper sweetened by the news of Drake's successes and his subsequent capture of the treasure galleon *St Phelipe*, Elizabeth dismissed the quarrel between the two men and promoted Burrough to the position of Controller of the Navy, based in the Thames Estuary far from Drake's home port of Plymouth. As for Drake, he was too great a man to carry on a vendetta against his former second-in-command.

Like his brother Stephen, William addressed himself to the instruction of ships' officers in the skills of seamanship. He published several books, notably *A Discourse of the Variation of the Compass.* He also applied himself to the pleasurable pursuit of 'getting a good wife for himself'. His choice alighted on the richly endowed granddaughter of a former Lord Mayor of London to whom he remained happily married for the rest of his life. In 1588, William sailed against the Spanish Armada, to which reference will be made later.

After a distinguished naval career, marred only by his quarrel with Drake, William Burrough died in 1599. His nephew, Christopher, carried on the Burrough brothers' underrated contribution to England's maritime history.

Following the failure to find the North-East Passage, another trade route to obtain the luxuries of the East remained to be pioneered – that of the old Viking route from Russia's White Sea in the frozen north to the tropical Caspian Sea, the Persian terminus from Cathay and the Orient.

On 19 June 1579, a Muscovy Company fleet, commanded by Arthur Edwards, aboard the *William and John*, sailed from Gravesend to St Nicholas on the White Sea on the first leg of a trading adventure to the Caspian. Christopher Burrough served as Russian interpreter. On arrival at St Nicholas, the cargo, which included Bideford kersey, a coarse woollen blanket cloth, was off-loaded on to river barks for the long journey down the Dvina River to Volgoda. From here, the Englishmen trekked overland to Yaroslav on the headwaters of the Volga River, from whence they sailed 2,000 miles southwards to Astrakhan, which they reached in October. After overwintering in the city, Christopher chartered a bark for the trading venture in the Caspian Sea, leaving Edwards behind to act as agent.

After navigating the complex channels of the Volga delta, the Englishmen reached the Caspian. Adverse winds carried their bark off course to the Asperon peninsula where Christopher dropped anchor. Going ashore at Baku, he presented his credentials to the Persian governor, who advised him to sail north to Derbend, the axis for oriental trade. At Derbend, Christopher completed successful trading deals in silks, spices, precious gems and prime yew staves for bows. Besides charting the Caspian coast, he kept a log of his impressions of the customs and politics of the countries he had visited. He noted that the people of Baku were fire worshippers and that Persian influence was declining while that of the Turks was being consolidated.

On his epic journey, he took aboard two Spaniards who had escaped from Tunisia, as well as other European refugees. After many adventures, the Englishmen returned to Astrakhan where they had to wait until late spring for the Volga to thaw. Laden with the proceeds of the Caspian enterprise, the *William and John* docked at Gravesend in September. Christopher Burrough did not return with the *William and John* but remained in northern Russia, supervising the Muscovy Company's trading interests.

With his love of the sea and seafaring men, it is inconceivable that young Richard Grenvile, son of Roger, the captain of the ill-fated *Mary Rose*, did not know of the exploits of the Burroughs of Northam, living as they all did in a tightly-knit maritime community where everybody knew everybody else's business. Young Richard spent his boyhood between the family estate at Stow, Kilkhampton, and their town house on Bideford quay, at the west end of the Longbridge.

Old Sir Richard died shortly after his release from his imprisonment after the Prayer Book War. Young Richard went to London to study law at the Inner Temple. While attending Court, he attracted the attention of Queen Elizabeth and soon became a favoured courtier on the fringe of the royal circle. In less romantic circumstances, he

Fig. 5. An early print of Bideford Quay. The donkey on the cobbled quay is harnessed to a truckle-mug, a Devon sledge.

came to the public notice when he became involved in a brawl with a rival gang of young bucks:

> They [the gangs] came together in an affray and when they were all fighting together, Grenvile ran through Banester with his sword, giving him a mortal wound six inches deep and one and a half in breadth of which he died within an hour afterwards. Thereupon the said Grenvile fled so that his goods and chattels lay under sentence of outlawry.

Elizabeth dismissed Banester's murder as an unfortunate consequence of aristocratic high spirits and after serving a short term of confinement Grenvile was released. With his 'goods and chattels' restored to him, he resumed his life at Court as though nothing had happened.

While a minor, Richard was returned as Member of Parliament for Dunheved – Launceston. In 1574, he negotiated a further Charter for Bideford whereby the town became a free corporate borough governed by a mayor, five aldermen, and seven burgesses. These officials formed a Common council from which a mayor was elected annually. The Charter consolidated the holding of a weekly market and the right to hold three fairs a year, and established a Court of Pie-Powder, a court with jurisdiction to administer summary justice to allcomers. Richard gave to the Borough the land on which stood the market, the future Guildhall and Allhallows Chapel. He also gave the land 'whereof certain limekilns sometimes stood and where a quay or wharf is laterly built; and also of all streets, lanes and ways within the said manor borough, and town of Bideford'. Not surprisingly Richard was elected Bideford's first senior alderman.

Young Richard led an adventurous life. He served as a mercenary officer in Hungary, fighting Turkish invaders. On his return to England, he joined a syndicate which intended to colonise Munster in South Ireland with Protestant settlers. In the 1560s he married Mary St Leger of Annerly, two-and-a-half miles upstream from Bideford. Although he had served as a soldier, Richard always yearned to go to sea and he numbered among his relatives and friends Sir Walter Raleigh, Humphrey Gilbert and Sir John Hawkins. In 1573, he purchased the heavily armed, 240-ton *Castle of Comfort*. From the Queen he obtained a patent granting him powers:

> to discover lands, territories, islands, dominions, people and places unknown which are not possessed by nor subject to, any Christian prince . . . and especially such as have the Pole Antarctic and the dominions of the great Cham of Cathay . . .

Elizabeth later cancelled the Patent and when she resurrected it, she gave it to her favourite, Sir Francis Drake.

Richard was appointed Sheriff of Cornwall in 1576. During his term of office, he arrested the Catholic priest, Cuthbert Mayne, who was born at Shirwell, near Barnstaple, and was latterly Rector of St Mary Magdalene, Huntshaw. He was sentenced to be hanged, drawn and quartered for the treasonable offence of wearing the banned Catholic emblem, the Agnus Dei, and for having received a Bill of Absolution from the Pope, and Grenvile supervised his execution in Launceston. Mayne was later to be canonised as a saint. At the end of his term of office, Richard received a knighthood.

In 1585, Richard led Sir Walter Raleigh's colonising expedition to North America. The Black Book of Plymouth notes that on 9 April, 'Sir Richard Grenvile, Knight, departed from Plymouth with VI ships and barks for Wingane Dehoy, where he carried VI men or thereabouts'. Grenvile flew his flag from the *Tiger*, 140 tons.

Distributed among the vessels of the small fleet were a hundred or so North Devon gentlemen with supplies to set up a new colony. On 20 June, the fleet made landfall on the coast of Florida. Sailing north, Grenvile disembarked the men at Roanoke in North Carolina to found a colony. On the homeward voyage, he captured the Spanish treasure ship, the *Santa Maria*.

The following year, he set sail from Bideford with supplies for Roanoke. Phillip Wyot, Barnstaple's town clerk, noted in his diary:

> 26 April. Sir Richard Grenvile sailed over Bideford Bar with his flyboat; but for want of sufficient water on the Bar, being near upon the neap, he left his ship. This Sir Richard pretended [intended] his going to Wyngandecora where he was last year.

When he eventually reached the settlement, Grenvile found that the surviving colonisers, after suffering many hardships, had been taken back to England by Sir Francis Drake. Having disembarked 15 settlers, he returned to Bideford. On the voyage he 'fell upon the Isle of Azores, on some of which islands he landed and spoiled all the towns of all such things as were worth carriage where also he took diverse Spaniards'.

From this North American expedition he brought back to Bideford a Wyngandtidoian Indian whom he had baptised and christened in the name of his cousin, Sir Walter Raleigh, at St Mary's church. The Register records: '1588. Cristunge Raleagh a Wyngantidoian baptised 27 of March'. Within a year the Indian was dead, killed by a combination of England's climate and lack of immunity against alien diseases.

Grenvile also brought home the cured leaves of the Indian Uppowoc plant, the importation of which was to be a cornerstone of Bideford's prosperity for years to come:

> In the West Indies Uppowoc hath divers names according to the several places and countries where it grows and is used; the Spaniards call it tobacco.

His cargo also included Indian clay smoking pipes which were to serve as models for Bideford pipemakers.

To facilitate the mobilisation of shipping at the time of war, the Admiralty compiled a register of all vessels of 100 tons or over. Among the West Country ships was a vessel of 250 tons built in Bideford for an Exeter merchant. In 1582, 150 shipmasters and 2,014 seamen were listed in Devon. A total of nine large ships based on Bideford and Northam reflected the growing importance of shipbuilding on Torridgeside.

By spring 1588, the threat of Spanish invasion had become imminent. On 1 April, the Lord Admiral ordered all West Country ships of 100 tons burden or over to be fitted out for war service. Of the six Bideford ships requisitioned, three, the *Dudley*,[1] *Virgin God Save Her* and the *Tiger*, belonged to Sir Richard Grenvile. These had already been victualled for a a voyage to America. Instead the ships were ordered to sail to Plymouth to join Sir Francis Drake's squadron. Sir Richard did not sail with the flotilla, but his son, John, commanded the *Tiger*. The remaining ships to be financed by Bideford, the *Victory* (250 tons), the *Bullett* and the *Bulldog* were retained for coastal defence in the Bristol Channel. In June 1588 the *Victory* engaged the Spanish fleet auxiliary, *San Juan*, in Bideford Bay. After a day-long battle the antagonists drifted apart. The next morning the battle resumed. With ammunition dangerously low, the *Victory* fired a double-charged broadside into the *San Juan*'s hull, forcing her to strike her colours. Triumphantly, the *Victory* towed her battered prize back to Bideford.

When shipping merchants holding lucrative privateering licences were warned that their ships were liable to be requisitiond for war service their patriotism – and that of their crews – became strained. Within days of receiving the Admiralty's instructions, the burghers of Bideford and Barnstaple pleaded that their towns were far too poor to

Fig. 6 Sir Richard Grenvile and Stephen Burroughs outside the *King's Arms*. Moored at the Quay is a replica of Drake's *Golden Hind*, built at Hunt's shipyard, Appledore.

shoulder the expense of maintaining the ships. They argued that their towns had suffered serious financial loss by being barred from trading with Spain, claiming this outlet was 'the only vent for all commodities arising among us by way of traffic'. Recent pirate attacks had lost them more ships than those captured as prizes. The towns' pleas fell on stony ground. The Lord Admiral dictated to the adjacent hundreds to help the two towns financially, threatening that if the money was not forthcoming, the Admiralty would fit out the vessels themselves and charge them with the bill. At the last moment, a local benefactor, George Norwood, put up the necessary capital.

Grenvile's ships arrived at Plymouth too late to take part in the English Channel battles with Medina Sidonia's Armada. After the Battle of Gravelines, in which Drake sent fire-ships among the anchored Spanish men-of-war, the weather deteriorated rapidly. For five days and nights a violent storm whipped up the Channel and all contact between the two fleets was lost. The Admiralty ordered William Burrough, then Controller of the Navy based on the Medway, to patrol the Thames Estuary in the last English-oared galleon, the *Bonovolia*. On sighting the enemy he was to signal their presence to the shore by cannon fire. Then he was to withdraw up the Thames and scuttle the aged *Bonovolia* in the shipping lane. As events transpired, the Spanish flight northwards went undetected. After suffering terrible privations, only a handful of fever-ridden Spanish ships limped back to Spain.

With the collapse of the invasion threat, a near bankrupt Treasury paid off the men of the Channel fleet then moored off the Kentish coast. Disease raged among the English crews. Sick seamen died in their dozens in the Cinque ports and surrounding countryside.

If Devon had witnessed the start of the great Elizabethan adventure, then Kent witnessed its miserable end. The indifference of the Queen to the plight of the discharged sailors helped to polarise the West Country attitudes in favour of the parliamentarians in the Civil War of 1642. However, Elizabeth, in recognition of the loyalty shown by the men of Torridgeside in the Armada's defeat, declared Bideford and Appledore to be free ports in perpetuity.

Bideford town council owns an iron-bound ship's chest[2] of the Armada period and a number of cannon claimed to be of Armada origin. Originally the barrels were sunk into the quayside for use as mooring bollards. When the quay was widened in the 19th century the corroded barrels were removed for preservation. Then, mounted on gun carriages, they were positioned outside the old Bideford School of Art. When the school was demolished to make way for the present post office the guns were given permanent positions in Victoria Park and Chudleigh's Fort at East-the-Water.

The Librarian of the Armoury of the Tower of London, Sarah Barter-Bailey, in May 1981, assessed the authenticity of the cannon:

> . . . as so often in these cases it is impossible to be definite in pronouncing on the date or origin of provenanced guns especially when they are as rusty as these are. I have, however, compared them with guns known to be of the 16th century . . . The best we can say is that . . . from their general outline, the guns in Victoria Park seem to be more likely to be 17th and even 18th century in date.

During the fateful summer of 1588, 16,000 trained men of Devon both Protestant and Catholic stood under arms prepared to repulse invading Spaniards. The County Marshal was responsible for recruitment, weaponry and training of the armed bands. Whilst under training, men received 8d. per mile up to six miles for transporting equipment to training areas at Buckland Brewer, Torrington and Woolfardisworthy (Woolsery). Failure to attend field training or omitting to return weapons was punishable by four days in jail. As workers were loth to forfeit wages and employers to lose production, training had to be restricted to half holidays and Sunday afternoons. Due to high cost, only at the end of his training was a musketeer permitted to fire a single bullet at a target.

The failure of the Armada in 1588 did not end the Spanish War. In 1590, Elizabeth recalled Sir Richard Grenvile, who was yet again trying to colonise Catholic Munster, to be second-in-command to Lord Thomas Howard's battle group of six warships, which had orders to sail to the Azores to ambush Spanish Admiral Don Alonso de Bazan's homeward-bound treaure fleet.

It was not the Spanish but the English who were caught napping off the Isle of Terceira, none more so than Sir Richard in his ship the *Revenge*. At the time 90 of the crew were suffering from fever. Sir Walter Raleigh, in his 'Report of the fight about the Isles of Azores', describes Grenvile's last epic fight:

> . . . many of our ships were on shore in the Island, some providing ballast for their ships, others filling of water and refreshing themselves from the land with such things as they could either for money, or by force recover . . . The Spanish fleet having shrouded their approach by reason of the Island; were no so soon at hand as our ships had scarce time to weigh their anchors. Sir Richard was the last weighed to recover the men that were upon the Island which otherwise had been lost.

After an exchange of gunfire, Lord Thomas, realising that the numerical superiority of the Spanish would overwhelm his fleet, ordered his ships to withdraw. Four captains complied with the order. But not Sir Richard. Instead he steered straight at the enemy line-of-battle. In the *Revenge*'s wake sailed the tiny *Foresight* which, after firing a few ineffectual rounds at the towering Spanish hulks, sensibly broke off the engagement. Now the *Revenge* stood alone to take on the combined might of de Bazan's warships. The 500-ton *Revenge* was both fast, immensely strong and highly manoeuvrable. In length 92 feet, 35 feet in beam and with a 15-ft. draught, she carried at the time of the battle 39 bronze cannon on two decks. Sir Francis Drake had considered her to be a perfect warship of her class.

The *Revenge*'s first attacker was the newest of Spain's Apostle-class galleons:

> The great *San Phelipe* being in the wind of him, and coming towards him becalmed his sails in such sort as the ship could neither weigh nor feel the helm; so huge and high charged was the Spanish ship being a thousand and five hundred tons.

Fortunately the *Revenge* possessed an advantage over her mighty opponent. With her guns set far lower in her hull than the enemy's, the English gunners were able to fire into the *San Phelipe*'s hull close to and below the waterline while most of the Spaniard's shot whistled over the *Revenge*'s decks. As the two ships became locked together, Spanish marines leapt aboard the *Revenge*. Hand to hand fighting raged. Then the *Revenge*'s gunners 'discharged with crossbar shot, the *San Phelipe* shifted herself with diligence from her sides, utterly misliking her first entertainment'. A galleon which came to the aid of the *San Phelipe* rammed the *Revenge*'s quarter deck with such force that the collision caused the Spaniard to beat a hasty withdrawal with water pouring through her splintered stem.

The unequal battle continued unabated:

> The Spanish ships were filled with companies of soldiers . . . After many interchanged volleys of great ordinance and small shot, the Spanish deliberated to enter the *Revenge* . . . but were still repulsed again and again and at all times beaten back into their own ships or into the sea but always others came in their places, she having never less than two mighty galleons by her side . . . so that ere morning, from three o'clock the day before, there had been several Armados assailed her; and alls so ill approved of their entertainment, as they were by the break of day, far more willing to harken to a composition, than hastily to make any more assaults or entries.

The *Revenge* had inflicted heavy losses on the enemy. During the night, the galleon *Ascension* and a badly damaged hulk had sunk.

Towards the end of the engagement, Grenvile received a headwound which was to prove fatal. The *Revenge*'s surgeon was dead. Forty of the crew had been killed and few of the remainder had come through the battle unscathed. The ship had sustained 88 hits, 14 holes being below the waterline. Sixteen feet of water in the holds had drowned the seriously wounded. Despite the sinking condition of the ship and the hopelessness of continuing the battle, Grenvile, oblivious to the pleas of the crew, refused to surrender. Instead he ordered the Master Gunner to use the last of the gunpowder to blow up the waterlogged ship. But he was no longer in charge of the situation. Other officers had already concluded an honourable surrender with de Bazan, and a Spanish boarding party took over the ship. They were appalled at the scenes of slaughter: 'The ship being marvellously unsavoury, filled with blood and bodies of the dead, and wounded like a slaughter house'.

They bore the dying Grenvile to de Bazan's flagship where the Spanish Admiral received his adversary, 'with all humanity, and left nothing unattempted that lended to his recovery, highly commending his valour and worthiness, and greatly bewailed the danger wherein he was . . .' Although he received the best medical attention, Grenvile died. Even in death, the Spanish seamen feared him:

> saying that as soon as they had threwn the dead body overboard, they verily thought that that he has a devilish faith and religion, and therefore the devil loved him.

Survivors of the *Revenge* were distributed among the Spanish ships. The *Revenge* was filled with both their own and English wounded for tranportation back to Spain. Then with the *Revenge* under tow, de Bazan's fleet set course for home.

As the Spaniards passed the Azores, a cyclone hit them. To the superstitious Spanish it seemed that Grenvile had indeed risen from the dead to wreak vengeance upon them. Over 20 of the flotilla were driven to destruction on the rocks of Terceira, or disappeared at sea. Ten thousand Spaniards perished in the disaster. The islanders were forbidden on pain of death to talk of the tragedy. As to the fate of the *Revenge*:

> She was cast upon a cliff near to the Isle of Terceira where it brake in a hundred pieces and sank to the ground having in her 70 Gallego's, Biscayan's and with some of the Englishmen whereof but one was saved that got up the cliffs alive and had his body and head all wounded, and being ashore brought us the news desiring to be shriven and thereupon died.

Over the following years, a trickle of survivors of the *Revenge* found their way home to Bideford. They brought with them Grenvile's dying words which are inscribed on a plaque beside the Lady Chapel in St Mary's church;

> Here die I, Sir Richard Grenvile, with a joyful and a quiet mind, for that I ended my life as a true soldier ought to do fighting for his Country, Queen, Religion, and Honour, my sould willingly departing from this body, leaving behind the lasting fame of having as every valiant soldier is bound to do.

When Bideford was granted armorial bearings in 1936, the town took as its motto a précis of these words, 'Bold for Queen and Country'.

There is an ironic twist to the epic of Grenvile's last fight. De Bazan's flotilla did not carry treasure, but a general cargo. Fast Spanish frigates laden with bullion sailed from Havana the following year, reaching Spain without incident.

Chapter Three

PIRACY AND CIVIL WAR (1603-1689)

IN 1603 QUEEN ELIZABETH died, leaving the country verging on bankruptcy. Under her successor, James I, the condition of England's already neglected navy deteriorated still further. Algerine and Salee pirates from the Mediterranean joined Dunkirkers in preying on English shipping. So rich and easy were the pickings off the Torridge estuary, Bideford Bay was dubbed the 'Golden Coast'.

Among the pirate captains who prowled the Bristol Channel was the flamboyant Thomas Salkheld, who seized Lundy Island and called himself king. During his reign of the island, Salkheld and his men captured several ships. Shaving the heads of his prisoners, he put them to work alongside islanders to build a quay and fortifications. After the completion of the work, Salkheld had a gallows set up, threatening to hang those who refused to swear allegiance to him. Leading a prisoners' revolt of 16 men and a boy, George Escott, a ship's officer from Appledore, put Salkheld and his henchmen to flight. In recognition of his action, Escott received a life pension of 8d. per day.

Salkheld's ignominious departure did not end the Lundy islanders' ordeal at the hands of pirates. In 1625, a Salee fleet took the island for a fortnight. After threatening to burn Ilfracombe, the Saleemen departed, taking with them all able-bodied islanders. Five years later English and Scottish buccaneers attempted to invade the island but were beaten back to their boats.

Even as far away as the Newfoundland cod banks, Bideford's fishing fleet, second only in number in Devon to that of Topsham, was not immune from molestation from pirates seeking both prizes and skilled crewmen. By 1636, western seaports had lost 87 ships valued at £100,000, while upwards of 3,000 Devonians had been captured.

An early benefit of Cromwell's Commonwealth (1646-59) to Bideford and other West Country ports was the strengthening of the navy. Re-equipped with fast, well-armed ships, the navy soon chased away the bulk of pirates infesting the Bristol Channel. Nevertheless sporadic raids continued albeit at a much reduced level.

Because of the difficulty in crewing naval ships, the Admiralty drafted press gangs into North Devon to round up experienced seamen. The gangs met with little success. In 1653, press-gang leaders Pen and Hewitt wrote from the *Golden Fleece*,[1] Barnstaple to their superiors in London that they had only managed to seize 40 men in Bideford and Barnstaple. To rectify the position the Admiralty directed Captain Henry Hatsell from Plymouth to North Devon. He complained he had:

> met with many obstructions, the merchants having procured an order from Council of State not to impress any belonging to ships bound for Newfoundland which carried away 300 men. Other vessels in Bideford Bar claimed the same privilege, though they had received orders for impressing. They gave fair words but no deeds. The power by which we act is questioned, and whether there be any such power at present, and the seamen are themselves with clubs and staves, and say if we take them it is at our peril, so that we are in great danger.

Refusal to collaborate with Hatsell did not stop Bideford and Barnstaple councils from appealing for naval protection when a sudden upsurge in piracy hit the Bristol Channel in 1653. The Council of State responded by despatching Captain Abra Algate in command of a frigate flotilla to Bideford Bay. He soon chalked up his first success by rescuing several vessels taken by a Brest privateer, which managed to escape. Three years later the mayors of Bideford, Barnstaple and Ilfracombe appealed to the council for frigates to be stationed in Bideford Bay in order to protect Irish shipping routes from Spanish interference.

Besides pirates, Bideford merchants faced another hazard to commerce, that of the Admiralty's failure to make prompt payment for goods and services. On 22 January 1656 Lionel Beecher, who had shipped army horses to Ireland in 1651, petitioned the Admiralty for the settlement of any even earlier account. He ended his letter with pathos to melt the stony Admiralty's heart:

> I have a wife and four children and have lately lost four ships taken by pirates of Brest so I shall be ruined unless you order some course for my necessities.

On 24 August 1666, the day on which the *St Katherine* of Riga sailed over Bideford Bar bound for Lisbon, the North Devon coast was declared free of pirates. That year Charles II had been on the throne for six years, having ended Oliver Cromwell's experiment in Republicanism. Twenty-four years earlier the country had been plunged into Civil War. Bideford, North Devon and most of the county of Devon stood solidly behind Cromwell's parliamentarians and against King Charles I.

The war was not long in coming to Devon. On 13 September, a recruiting party of royalist gentry descended on South Molton and were met by a hostile reception from the townsfolk. A royalist commentator reported that:

> . . . I do verily believe they were in number at least 1,000 some with halberts and black bills, some with clubs, some with pikes some with dung evells . . . The women had filled all the steps of the cross with great stones and got up and sat on them, swearing if they did come near they would brain them. One thing is worth noting, a butcher's wife, came running with her lapful of rams-horns for to throw at them. Some of the gentlemen were coming towards the Cross . . . the people did give a great shout, and they did cry, 'They be come', at which they were ready to stand against them, the Gentlemen seeing that, betook themselves everyone to house, and after that not one of them nor their servants, durst show themselves in the street . . .

At the first opportunity, a force of royalist cavalry, including Sir Ralph Hopton who was to render distinguished service to the King in the west country, found themselves in enemy countryside. Turning westwards, the Cavaliers rode to Kilkhampton, and the Stow estate of Sir Bevil Grenvile, grandson of Sir Richard of the *Revenge*. Sir Bevil, a kingsman to the core, had already mortgaged his Manor of Bideford, including Lundy Island, for £3,000 to help raise £20,000 to keep 300 men under arms.

The people of Bideford looked to the defence of the town. Twenty-five-year-old Colonel James Chudleigh, an officer of the Barnstaple garrison, supervised the building of twin gun bastions to protect the Longbridge; one on high ground at East-the-Water, the other, the site of which has since disappeared, on the west bank of the Torridge. Another fort, at Staddon Hill, Appledore, guarded the Torridge estuary.

Fig. 7.   Bull Hill, possibly the site of Chudleigh's west bank Civil War fort. The tower in the background is a Victorian belvedere.

During the winter of 1642, Sir Ralph Hopton, now commanding royalist forces besieging Exeter, anticipated a parliamentarian attack from North Devon. He despatched Colonel Ackland and Sir Bevil Grenvile to capture the strategically-important hilltown of Torrington. The men of Bideford and Barnstaple then marched on the town to expel them. In the fighting, both sides claimed success.

In late January, Bidefordians joined a parliamentarian army led by James Chudleigh on a campaign to raise the siege of Plymouth. At Chagford, their scouting parties came up against royalist troops. Many of the ill-armed parliamentarians threw away their *rusticke* weapons and fled. In the ensuing chase, the royalists captured 140 prisoners and took 30 pack animals laden with ammunition and food. But a few rebels stood their ground – a Barnstaple sniper shot down Sir Sydney Godolphin, the poet and Colonel of the King's Horse.

Displaying remarkable resilience, Chudleigh's men reformed and resumed their march. They remained several days in the Totnes area practising battle drill before joining the main parliamentarian concentration at Kingsbridge. Seizing the Avon river bridge at Aveton Gifford on 20 February, the parliamentarians established a bridgehead on the western bank thereby threatening Modbury and the Plymouth road.

At dawn on the 21st, the parliamentarians broke out of the bridgehead and after fierce fighting they captured Modbury. Its capture cost them seven dead while the royalists lost 100 men killed, 200 wounded and 100 taken prisoner. In their flight, the royalists abandoned five cannon and 1,000 muskets. Meanwhile, Plymouth's defenders launched a successful surprise attack against Hopton's Cornish infantry. The siege of Plymouth had been raised, and the royalists had suffered a humiliating defeat. In London, the news of the parliamentarian victory was greeted with peals of church bells and rejoicing in the streets. The two sides negotiated an uneasy truce. Sir Bevil agreed to withdraw his men to Stow while the Bideford and Barnstaple contingents returned to their towns.

The royalists did not take long to break the truce. On 12 April, Sir Bevil hatched a plot to take Bideford by stealth.

> He sent some of his soldiers into the town like countrymen . . . who confederated themselves with some of the malevolent townsmen, to surprise the watch of the Town and to cut their throats on a certain night, and then an alarm should be given by them as a call to the rest of Sir Bevil's regiment which should have attended near to the Town to have come in to their aid and finished the exploit; but it pleaed God in his merciful providence to discover the treachery thus; one of the conspirators being a Townsman happened to be drunk the afternoon before the dismal night and in his drunkeness openly babbled out what feats he and the rest of his accomplices meant to perform the night following, which being taken of and thoroughly examined, and all the conspirators were instantly apprehended together with all Sir Bevil's soldiers thatnd thoroughly examined, and all the conspirators were instantly apprehended together with all Sir Bevil's soldiers that were then in the town and their persons secured and committed to safe custody to receive condign punishment according to their demerits.

If Sir Bevil had banked on the support of the townspeople, he had misjudged his popularity in Bideford. A contemporary letter stated: 'Sir Bevil Grenvile hath been a tyrant, especially by his tenants, threatening to thrust them out of the house and home if they will not assist him and his confederates'.

A threat to the north Devon rebels was averted when a Welsh barque, attempting to smuggle bullion and 500 muskets to royalist sympathisers, was captured in Bideford Bay. The cache was escorted to Exeter for use by the rebel garrison.

Now the royalists had broken the truce, Bidefordians prepared to resume the war.

James Chudleigh, promoted to the rank of Sergeant-Major-General and commanding an army of 5,000 North Devonians, marched to block the advance of royalist forces. Near Okehampton, 1,500 Bideford and Barnstaple sailors arrived to reinforce his army. Fearing for the safety of the Taw and Torridge ports Chudleigh urged them to return home and 'make good Bideford and Barnstaple'.

Chudleigh's army came into contact with the royalists at Stourton Down on 24 April.[2] The parliamentarian force had become dangerously weakened and hundreds of men had drifted back home. The transport train had broken down and the artillery was virtually immobilised by lack of dray horses. Chudleigh was not to know that the majority of Hopton's Cornish infantry, after months of campaigning, were in bad shape, many verging on starvation, and in no condition to fight a battle.

On a stormy night in which thunder rumbled over the moorland and lightning speared down on Dartmoor, Chudleigh made his dispositions. He urged his men on no account to give their positions away by opening fire prematurely on the advancing royalists. Unfortunately, a rifleman accidentally discharged his weapon. In the darkness, the royalists formed up for battle. A rebel cavalry attack threw royalist cavalry into confusion. Chudleigh urged his infantry forward. The enemy foot soldiers broke and fled. Only the royalist artillery offered resistance, but they too were forced to abandon their guns and disappeared into the darkness.

The thunderstorm, which had threatened for so long, broke over the Down. It appeared to the royalists that the Almighty had turned against them. When a rebel cavalryman mounted on a black horse loomed out of the darkness, the royalists were convinced the rider was the devil himself. To make matters worse, a parliamentarian witness wrote:

> The Lord sent Fire from Heaven so that the Cavaliers powder in their bandoliers, flasks, and muskets took fire by which means they hurt and slew each other to the wonder and amazement of the Parliament forces.

This weird phenomenon, caused by the electric storm, completely unnerved the royalists who fled the moor, leaving behind a mass of booty including Hopton's muster rolls, lists of royalist sympathisers, and two coded messages from the King.

Dispirited royalists, many suffering from powder burns, crowded into nearby Launceston. The parish register notes: 'sending three militia men by a pass into Devon that had been scalded . . . 6d.'. The parliamentarians had stemmed the royalist invasion, but not for long. Royalist fugitives joined up with a new army being raised in Cornwall. Within days of the débâcle at Stourton Down, the royalists went over to the offensive. On 15 May they marched out of Launceston to link up with Hopton's and Grenvile's army stationed at Stow.

The parliamentarians were also on the move northwards. From information decoded from a message found in Hopton's portmanteau, the Earl of Stamford, parliamentarian commander in the west, ordered Chudleigh to proceed to north Cornwall to counter a threatened seaborne attack from Wales. On 16 May the rival armies faced each other a mile north of Stratton.

Chudleigh's army occupied Grist Hill,[3] a strong defensive position dominating the Stratton – Stibb road. On the plateau of the precipitous escarpment, rebel pioneers had thrown up earthworks where cannoneers and riflemen were positioned to bring down fire on royalists trying to scale the heights. Except for artillery, the rebels had an overwhelming numerical superiority over the royalists.

Hopton attacked the hill at dawn on 16 May. Time and time again royalists toiled up the rocky escarpment only to be thrown back by the defenders. By mid-afternoon, the battle had reached its crisis point. The royalist artillery were down to their last five barrels of powder, sufficient to support a final attack. Keeping the shortage a secret, Hopton and Grenvile led an assault on the hill with every available man. The rebels had only to stand their ground until the enemy gunners had expended their powder. Then the royalist infantry would be at their mercy, and the Battle of Grist Hill would be an even greater victory than that of Sourton Down.

As the royalists neared the crest of the hill, the rebels launched a counter attack in which Sir Bevil was nearly killed and Chudleigh captured. Deprived of Chudleigh's leadership, the rebels' resistance collapsed. The disaster at Grist Hill cost them 300 dead with 1,700 taken prisoner. All their cannon was captured together with 70 barrels of gunpowder, and a large haul of food.

The King honoured Sir Ralph Hopton with the Baronetcy of Stratton. Sir Bevil's grandson later placed a commemorative plaque on the battlefield.[4] Sir Bevil could claim the rare distinction of having played a crucial role in a major battle fought in the parish of his birth. As for James Chudleigh, the Earl of Stamford was convinced he had not been captured but had defected to the enemy. The Earl also poured scorn on Chudleigh's leadership in the fighting. Later James Chudleigh persuaded his father to switch his allegiance to the King's cause. James, now a royalist officer, died in the siege of Dartmouth later in the year. Hopton and Grenvile's forces advanced out of Devon and Somerset. To ensure Bideford's subjugation, royal commissioners directed George Chappell, commanding *The Hope of Topsham*, to blockade the Torridge estuary.

In June, Sir Bevil died from wounds sustained during the Battle of Lansdowne, Bath. In his pocket was found a letter patent from King Charles granting him the earldom of Bath. His body was taken back to Kilkhampton by his devoted servant, Anthony Payne, the giant of Stratton, for interment in the family vault. With Bevil's death and the break up of the family's extensive estates, the Grenvile influence on Bideford declined.

Despite being blockaded from the sea and threatened on land, the Bideford parliamentarians launched an offensive against royalist skirmishers who were terrorising the countryside. They joined men of Barnstaple and Torrington in a punitive operation in Cornwall to seize 'the estates and goods of such of the Cornish Cavaliers as now besiege Exeter, endeavouring by that means to draw them from the city, to look to the safety of their own substance at home'.

Reprisal raids against their properties by a peasant rabble was a situation no royalist gentleman would tolerate. In order to smash the rebels, Col. John Digby, with a regular cavalry regiment based in the Torrington area, received substantial reinforcements. The rebels reacted to the threat with a recklessness which was bound to end in disaster. Under the command of Captain Bennet, a soldier of fortune, men of Bideford and Barnstaple mustered at Huntshaw and Gammaton Cross to march on Torrington. Barnstaple provided 370 infantry, 130 cavalry and two cannon while the Bideford contingent provided 500 infantry and 200 horse. This force of badly trained men were to take on Digby's 1,800 disciplined infantry and cavalry.

Such a large enemy force could not be assembled without Digby's knowledge. In good time, he planted an ambush in the wooded valley of the Norwood stream. In the early afternoon, royalist observers on the tower of St Michael's church spotted the parliamentarian vanguard approaching the stone bridge over the stream.

The rebels entered the royalists' trap totally unprepared for the musket fire which cut into their ranks. Panic stricken survivors fled back up the road to become entangled with the main rebel column. Into this mêlée, Digby's cavalry rode with sabres slashing. Throwing down their weapons, the rebels struggled to escape from the slaughter. Their cavalry took flight leaving the foot to the tender mercies of Digby's men. Fugitives were chased back to the Bideford defences. For the loss of one man dead, the royalists had inflicted another shattering defeat on the rebels.

With the return of the survivors of the Norwood massacre, Bidefordians knew that their town would be Digby's next objective. Digby lost no time in pressing home his advantage. Firstly, the royalists stormed Chudleigh's fort at Staddon Heights, Appledore, and then Bideford came under close scrutiny. The people of Barnstaple managed to ship essential supplies to their beleaguered neighbours in an effort to boost their resistance. However, it was not direct royalist assault but the activities of fifth columnists within which brought about the fall of both towns.

By winter 1645, the tide of war had turned against the royalists. After liberating Bristol and routing royalists at Langport, General Sir Thomas Fairfax and Lt.-Gen. Oliver Cromwell's parliamentarians invaded Devon. Before dawn on 14 December, the 10,000 strong Parliamentary army entered Winkleigh. Hopton's stronghold at Torrington was barely a day's march away.

Early the next morning, the parliamentarians began their advance on Torrington. After fierce skirmishing at Stevenstone House, the royalists retired in good order to the town's defensive perimeter. There the infantry took up prepared positions with a cavalry force in support. Hopton had stationed reserve cavalry on the northern common and also within the earthworks of the old castle. Infantry units were dispersed in the side streets. No mention is made of either side employing artillery in the fighting.

Whereas cavalry numbers were approximately equivalent, Hopton's infantry was numerically inferior. Moreover their battle worthiness had been sapped by defeat, hunger and atrocious weather conditions. In spite of this disadvantage, Hopton and his second-in-command Digby formed a redoubtable leadership.

When darkness fell, Fairfax called a halt to the advance. His forward positions ran within four fields distance from the heavily defended turnpike. Around midnight, Fairfax and Cromwell made an inspection of their lines. Detecting enemy activity, Fairfax sent a patrol to investigate. Before the patrol reached its objective, royalists opened fire. Without waiting for orders, parliamentarian cavalry galloped to their comrades' assistance. Cromwell called up reinforcements and what had begun as a localised incident rapidly grew into a general engagement along the length of the royalist defences.

Remorselessly the parliamentarians wore down the royalist resistance and increasing numbers surrendered or deserted. When the turnpike fell Hopton's cavalry reserve launched a desperate counter attack which threw the rebels back to their start line, but here the thrust petered out for lack of support. Fairfax immediately retaliated with a cavalry charge which swept aside Hopton's horse. In the fighting, Hopton received a pike wound in the face while Digby's horse was killed under him.

It was at this critical stage of the battle that Torrington was rocked by a violent explosion. Eighty kegs of gunpowder stored in the crypt of St Michael's church had exploded. In the main body of the church were 200 rebel prisoners and 20 guards. The majority were killed instantly and nearby dwellings were either destroyed or set on fire. Fairfax himself narrowly missed death when lead sheets, blasted from the church roof, fell within a few feet of him.

The explosion came to the superstitious as a sign of heavenly displeasure. Royalists threw away their weapons and equipment and fled the town while the bulk of the cavalry retreated to the Taddyport Bridge over the River Torridge. Other horsemen made their escape over the Rothern Bridge. Foot-guards who had held out on Castle Green slithered down the precipitous hill to the river where Fairfax's cavalry could not catch them. A substantial royalist contingent retreated through Weare Giffard to Bideford where they crossed the Longbridge on their flight to Cornwall. In the convoy were 'two considerable persons carried in horse-litters groaning and crying out in pain'. By dawn the last royalist soldier had quit Torrington. Now came the task of probing through the church's ruins for survivors. One of those pulled out alive was a desperate character named Watts who claimed that the royalists had paid him £30 to blow up the church. Fairfax gave his soldiers a few days' rest before liberating Bideford and Barnstaple. But with the end of the fighting, there came a far more dreadful ordeal to bear – the bubonic plague.

During June 1646 a Spanish merchantman unloaded a cargo of merino wool on Bideford quay. The fleeces had been imported to be woven with coarser Devon wool to produce the soft Bideford 'Perpetuano'. Henry, John and Christopher, sons of Henry Ravening, surgeon of Allhalland Street, with a friend, Hugh Caldwell, played among the bales unaware that the fleeces were infected by bubonic-infected rat fleas.[5] Within the space of a few days, all the boys were dead, their blood poisoned by the bites of the deadly parasites. A plaque in the parish church to the memory of the Ravening brothers reads:

> In memory of Henry, John and Christopher
> Ravening of this Towne, Surgione, 1646.
> To whom God lends
> Fair wings to fly
> Our trust needs them in God must be
> Our age was young, our age was tender
> We were three Ravens
> That here be under.

A headstone recovered from the cemetery, worded with chilling brevity, recorded the death of another victim:

> George Forgitt,
> In the diseas died here.

From Allhalland Street, the plague streaked through the town's squalid and insanitary hovels 'diffusing itself to so shocking a degree, the houses were filled with horror, and the streets covered in grass'. Among the wealthy citizens who fled the town at the outbreak of the plague was the mayor whose name 'has deservedly sunk into oblivion'.

The heroes of the pestilence were men of the calibre of Henry Ravening and John Strang of Ford House, a wealthy merchant and oftimes mayor of Bideford. Strang had led a charmed life. As a boy, he had survived a cliff fall while bird-nesting, and was later permanently scarred by an arrow wound to the head. He survived an attack from a footpad who threw him into the Torridge from the Longbridge. Now, on his own

Fig. 8. Merchant's House in Allhalland
Street. The bubonic plague of 1646 spread
from this area to the rest of the town.

initiative, he took upon himself the most dangerous job of his life, that of administering
the plague-ridden town.

To prevent the plague spreading, Strang posted sentries on all roads to stop and turn
back people either trying to enter or leave the town. In conjunction with Dr. Ravening,
he visited the sick and arranged for the collection and burial of the dead; 'he performed
even other offices of the good Christian, the vigilant magistrate'. Inevitably, John
Strang, the man whom the ordinary townsfolk believed Providence had sent to save
them from the plague, contracted the 'sore Fever' and died in July 1646. A shipwrecked
sailor who had once received help and friendship from Strang placed a monument in
St Mary's church dedicated to his benefactor's memory. On his own death, the sailor
bequeathed properties in Meddon Street to house poor people of the town.

During the seven months in which the plague raged in Bideford, 229 registered deaths
were attributed to the pestilence. After the plague had abated, Dr. Ravening and his
wife moved to Barnstaple where their daughter, Rebekah, was born.

In 1685, the West Country was once again plunged into civil war. During June,
James Scott, Duke of Monmouth, affectionately known as 'Gaffer Scott', landed at
Lyme Regis to claim the English throne from his brother, the unpopular James II.
Among Monmouth's followers was Major Nathaniel Wade, a professional gunnery
officer.

Monmouth's rebellion stood little chance of success. While the majority of the landed

Fig. 9. Old Ford House, New Road, the town's oldest house. Mr. Strang, one of
Bideford's plague heroes lived here.

gentry were aware that negotiations to depose the popish James in favour of William
of Orange were well advanced, they made little attempt to warn ordinary West Country
Protestants from joining Gaffer Scott's vagabond army. For a month the rebels, including
Samuel Potts of Bideford, meandered through the West Country pursued by royalist
troops. At the Battle of Sedgemoor in the Somerset wetlands, the rebels were crushed.
Three hundred rebels died in the fighting, 1,000 died in the pursuit and dozens of
prisoners were executed without trial. Samuel Potts, who had a close family relationship
with Bideford, was among those captured and later executed at Honiton. Major Wade
escaped the carnage and made for the Bristol Channel with other fugitives.

King James sent Judge Jeffreys to the west to conduct 'show' trials of prisoners. These
notorious trials became known as the 'Bloody Assizes'. At Taunton, Jeffreys had the
professional services of the London executioner, Jack Ketch, and his assistant, Pasha
Rose, to hang, draw and quarter the condemned. A local character rejoicing in the
name of Tom Boilman officiated at the seething pots where the quarters and heads were
boiled and pickled in pitch.

Deputy Sheriff Thomas Mortimore had the responsibility for distributing and exhibit-
ing the gruesome remains in Devon. In a letter to his superior, Richard Coffin of
Portledge, he listed the towns in which the quarters were to be shown. Included was
Bideford where quarters were to be suspended in several parts of the town 'to the
disgrace of humanity and to the great inconvenience of the inhabitants'. In a letter to
Coffin, Mortimore warned:

> . . . the quarters are already boiled and tarred; warrants are to be sent to the Mayor to set them up.
> I saved you considerably by my journey to Wells, and endeavour to save you what expenses I can;
> however it is exceeding chargeable and troublesome, another years trouble will I not undertake for
> £500 . . .

Later Mortimore was to write: 'We are about to send quarters of rebels and those to be whipped at Torrington, Barnstaple, Bideford and some to Plymouth'. His death in the following year from 'lurking fever' saved him from further such macabre duties.

In the wake of the rebellion, dragoons commanded by Sir Richard Grenvile put Bideford under martial law. All males had to swear oaths of allegiance to James. Whilst stationed in the town, Dragoon John Craford died on 11 May 1688.

Major Wade, now a war criminal with a price on his head, evaded the royalist dragnet, and reached the North Devon coast. Here his luck ran out. Cornered near the home of Farmer Howe and his wife at Brendon, Somerset, who had given him shelter regardless of their own safety, Wade made an abortive attempt to escape. Gravely wounded by a pistol shot, he received treatment from Dr. Nicholas Cooke who was joined later by Dr. Henry Ravening, Bideford's plague doctor, now in the twilight of his life. Despite the gravity of the wound, the doctors extracted the bullet lodged close to Wade's lungs and stemmed the haemorrhage. But Wade's condition remained critical and the doctors, fearing for his life, sought the King's instructions for the disposal of his body should he die:

> We desire to know his Majesty's pleasure what we should do with his corpse, if he dies, which if he does before you answer we think to disembowel him. We will do what is possible we can, for he has assured us . . . he will make a full discovery of all he knows, but not by merits his pardon.

That Wade survived the surgery and escaped post-operative infection speaks highly of the professional competence of Cooke and Ravening. Wade escaped execution, as did the Howes who sheltered him. He never forgot Mrs. Howe's bravery and he settled a generous annuity upon her. Henry Ravening, Bideford's plague doctor, died on 12 February 1689.

Chapter Four

SEWERS, WARS AND SHIPWRECKS (1673-1801)

EARLY 17th-CENTURY BIDEFORD could in no way be compared to the 'little white town' eulogised by Charles Kingsley in his novel *Westward Ho!*. In common with other English towns during the Middle Ages Bideford was dirty and smelly, and for ordinary people, life was short, nasty and brutal. Rich and poor, merchant and monger were all guilty of contributing to the insanitary conditions. In 1673, Bideford council issued the following statement:

> This Court taking into serious consideration the great danger that the inhabitants of this town may be in as to their bodily health by noisome and stinking dunghills and other filth which too frequently has been cast out in hedges, in several streets and on the Quay of this Town, and suffered to lie long there, whereby the Air, especially in summer time, is apt to be corrupted, and hog and swines have been permitted to run up and down the town, which does also greatly conduce to breed diseases in the bodies of men, women and children inhabiting and residing in the Town; for preventing of such diseases as much in the Court lists, and remedying of such evil practices in the future . . .

To help alleviate the situation, the council undertook to position barrels in various parts of the town for the collection of rubbish. The town scavengers had orders to empty these at regular intervals.

Among those brought before the court was Abraham Heaman who was accused of having a dung heap at his front door on the quay. Hugh Langdon not only had a heap by his back door, but allowed his pigs to wander about the town, rooting in dung heaps. The town scavenger, Christopher Joynt, was censured for failing to remove a dung heap from against a wall belonging to the Earl of Bath, Lord of the Manor, and another by the Old Market House. The Earl was in constant trouble with the court. He was found responsible for having a malodorous pit under the Bow, a dangerous wall on the north side of Mary Sander's house in Bridge Street, an unmended fence adjoining John Atkey's garden in Bath Street, leading from Buttgarden Street to the High Street, and a dung heap near Elizabeth Buse's house in the High Street.

The dangers of disastrous fires in the town concentrated the attention of the court. Thomas and Gabriel Beale and Philip Whitson of Potter's Lane[1] were reprimanded for keeping bundles of furze stacked against their homes. Potters had to limit their kindling to 300 bundles which had to be kept at least 240 feet from their kilns. Bakers and brewers were restricted to 100 bundles to be kept at least 150 feet from their premises.

Over the years, the council continued to complain of the nuisance of pigs running amok. Richad Sleeper, blacksmith, and Roger Wilbraham, wardens of the parish

36

church, were found guilty of allowing pigs to feed in the churchyard. Thomas Michelson, Peter Bagehole and John Clotworthy were cited as incorrigible rogues.

Another bye-law concerned the maintenance of ditches and the cutting of roadside hedges. Thomas Lake was censured for allowing the ditches between Bowden Green and Handy Cross near *Le Tweenawayes*[2] to fall into disrepair. For not cutting their hedges, the following appeared before the magistrates: Valentine Pode, for hedges outside the Old Leys leading to Littleham; John Gennett, for hedges near Jacob's Cross; John Cawsey, for hedges by the Littleham road; John Davie jnr., and Thomas Rowe for hedges towards the long meadow; Henry Belcher, for hedges by the road to Rawley Ford; Robert Wickett, for hedges on the Torrington Road.

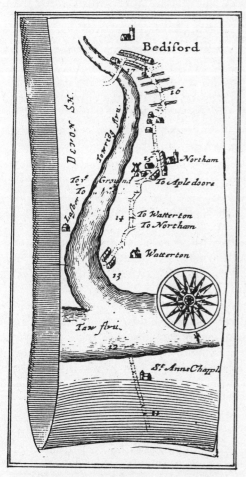

Fig. 10. The Bideford-Northam road, from Ogilby's *Traveller's Guide*, 1699.

By the end of the 17th century Bideford had entered the period of its greatest prosperity. Fortunes were made by enterprising tobacco merchants like the Davys and Bucks, and the new wealthy demanded a higher standard of living. Consequently, solidly built houses replaced the less substantial and insanitary homes of old. Removed from the smoky stench of the town nucleus, the Longbridge Trustees bought land on the northern edge of the town to build a street for long leasehold merchants' residences. By the end of the century, fine residences designed by Nathaniel Gascoyne lined both sides of a wide and elegant street – Bridgeland Street. Probably the most imposing and best preserved of these homes is No. 28, built for William Buck, instantly recognisable from the street by its guttering with the initials H.I.E. picked out in gold leaf. The house has changed little since its completion in the 1690s. A street door leads to a cobbled courtyard. In the yard, a well provided drinking water for the house. A large walled garden ensured both privacy and supplies of fresh vegetables. A shippon for milch cows, beehives, chicken coops and pig styes gave the household a measure of self-sufficiency.

Affixed to the house's wall is an indestructible iron plaque indicating that the house was insured against fire. Perhaps the most enigmatic of Bideford's historic relics is a milestone with the weatherworn inscription:

7
MILES
TO
NEW YORK FERRY
17..

To coincide with the building of Bridgeland Street, the quay was extended by 200 feet for the mooring of ships owned by the merchants of the street which became the hub of the town's tobacco and fish trade. When the stench of rotting fish became intolerable, even to noses inured to the town's smells, magistrates took action to rectify the nuisance. In 1680, the court ordered Alderman Thomas Gearing to remove barrels of bad fish from the cellars of his house in Bridgeland Street.

Fig. 11.   Strand House, an 18th-century merchant's house.

At the eastern end of the Longbridge, John Davie built himself an imposing mansion, parts of which, including an impressive staircase, survive in the *Royal Hotel*. Davie later moved away from the smoke and hassle of commercial Bideford to the country seclusion of Orleigh Court,[3] Buckland Brewer.

Little documentation remains of early shipbuilding and ancillary industries on Torridgeside. In 1540, the chronicler Leland describes the town as consisting of a 'Praty quik streat of smithies and other occupiers for ship craft'. The slow growth of shipbuilding prior to the 16th century arose from a bureaucratic anomaly whereby Barnstaple dominated the mouth of the Torridge through its control of Appledore. Bideford's shipping could not reach the open sea or its associated 'creeks' of Clovelly and Hartland without first obtaining clearance from Appledore's Custom House, a long-winded procedure. After years of negotiations between the two towns, commonsense prevailed. In the 1670s, a royal warrant awarded Bideford control of Appledore, thereby giving her unrestricted access to the open sea. From thence onwards shipbuilding on the Torridge boomed, so much so that the town was put forward as a candidate for development as the most important naval dockyard in the west. This unlikely scheme came to nothing, even though its backers were thought to have been local magnates who had the ear of the Admiralty. However, lesser industries carried on, including lime burning and the extraction of Bideford Culm, a low grade carboniferous mineral which provided black pigment for paint used in waterproofing ships' timbers. Paint mines were worked at East-the-Water, Pitt Lane and off Meddon Street.

By the middle of the century, deterioration of the Longbridge gave the Trustees cause for grave concern. In essential repairs carried out in 1638, the parapets were raised to 4ft. 5in. to give greater protection to foot traffic. Later the Trustees had a sundial and other ornamentation costing £27 10s. 0d. incorporated on the bridge.

In 1617, the Trustees leased to Richard Dunnying a bakehouse in Allhalland Street for the purpose of enlarging the grammar school founded by the Grenviles sometime in the late 16th or early 17th century.

Bideford, now staunchly Protestant, had won an enviable reputation for giving haven to persecuted religious sects. In St Mary's churchyard is a gravestone dedicated to the Greening family who had fled from Gloucester in 1666 at 'a time of great persecution for conscience's sake'. The parish register identifies 90 or so Huguenot families, refugees from French Catholic oppression who settled in the area between 1685 and 1720. Dissenting Bidefordians were liable to prosecution under the Conventicle Act. John Bartlett, son of a late vicar of St Mary's, was caught conducting an illegal service in the home of Miss Sarah Dennis. Sarah and Bartlett were fined £20 while the worshippers were fined 5s.0d. each. Twenty-three persons were arrested at the house of Samuel Johns and had to pay a combined total of £46 5s. 0d. in fines.

Bideford has had its share of controversial parish priests, none more so than the Rev. Michael Ogilby who interrogated the Bideford witches (see Appendix Two). In 1679, the court jurors had justifiable reasons to be disturbed by Ogilby's erratic behaviour:

> We do present that the said Michael Ogliby on Sunday, 8th Oct, in the Parish Church, as Mr John Hill, Town Clerk was going out of Church after morning prayer did rail and bestow very much railing and unchristian language upon the said John Hill, holding out his staff, threatening and assaulting of him therewith.
> We do present that the said Mr Ogilby for the space of 3 or 4 years now past has been, and still does continue to be a man very much given to railing and villifying of the Reverent Clergy of Parishes within the County of Devon, and of Magistrates, especially those of the Town of Bideford, as also for being a very great drinker, and immoderate lover of wine and strong drink, even of ebriety, also in the time aforesaid has been very many times guilty of profane and dreadful swearing . . . [he] had broken the ancient customs of the Parish and Town of Bideford by demanding, extorting and receiving of and from several of the inhabitants and parishioners, unreasonable, immoderate, and unjust fees or sums of money for marrying, baptising and burials.

Ogilby's irascibility was matched by bricklayer Richard Allen who was bound over on 18 April to be of good behaviour for abusing the rector the previous Sunday in church.

Since Elizabethan times, inns had been subject to licensing and supervision by local magistrates and the town's constables. Closing times generally coincided with the curfew. Many publicans brewed their own beer, the price of which varied between 1½d. and 4d. per gallon according to strength and quality. In 1676, Bideford magistrates granted 45 licences representing a public house for every 60 head of population. Fifteen licencees were women. Publicans set up ale-stakes, the forerunner of the pub sign, to advertise their premises. Those who infringed the licensing laws were dealt with by the magistrates. Widow Rebecca Lang fell foul of the law for keeping 'inmates of ill rule in her house', and lost her licence. Margaret Daines was 'suppressed for selling ale' and bound over to be of good behaviour for a similar offence. Gaming regulations were strictly enforced. Henry Belcher, a common tavern keeper, was summoned for allowing shove ha'penny to be played on his premises to the annoyance of his neighbours. Robert Knolman, Thomas Michelson, Samuel Gabriell, Peter Cockhill, John Clotworthy, Thomas Webber, Thomas Whitfield, Andrew Croote, Elizabeth Yeo and William Moore were found guilty of permitting the unlawful game of nine pins – skittles – to be played in their gardens.

Besides the licensed premises, illegal boozing dens flourished. In 1673, Henry Belcher was fined for selling ale without a licence. Drunkenness was common among both sexes and even among children. The court declared Peter Bagehole, tailor, to be a common drunkard. Thomas Bedford, landwaiter, was convicted for being drunk and fined 5s.0d. John Saunders of Abbotsham, tailor, and Matthew Knill, mason, were apprehended for tippling in Robert Poole's house. The fine of 2s.0d. was given to the overseers of the poor. Peter Baglehole was again in trouble at Christmas 1677, when the court fined him 5s.0d. for being drunk, 'and being the second conviction – though he oftentimes escaped', he was bound over to be of good behaviour.

Every *bona fide* resident of a parish had a claim upon that parish for relief in case of need. Those found living without permission in a different parish to their domicility were expelled. Unemployed Elinor Mugford of Hartland, living with William Ford, was warned to be out of the town within seven days. Richard Harrison of Bideford omitted to obtain a pass to Shebbear, and was sent home by the parish watchman. Bideford watchmen denied entry to pedlars and 'petty chapmen' travelling without official documentation.

Single women who bore illegitimate children had to appear before the court to satisfy the magistrates that their offspring would not become a burden on the parish. William Thomas, uncle of Margaret Noble, spinster, gave a security bond to the mayor exempting the parish for any responsibility towards his niece's 'base child of the male sex'. Found guilty in 1679 of 'bastardy, at least [sexual] incontinence, hardly escaping bigamy', Mary Gay was bound over to be of good behaviour.

The magistrates appointed watchdogs to examine the quality of goods for sale in the town. The Searchers and Sealers of Leather, Philip Bowden and Miles Duff, seized shoes manufactured in Stratton and Torrington for having an 'insufficiency of leather'.

In 1674, the mayor was reprimanded for allowing the town hall to become neglected. He was also censured for failing to weigh the bread and test the weights and measures, as well as omitting to have posted the table of fees. In 1687-8, the council published proclamations banning the importation of cheap foreign needles and buttons.

The council interested itself in the progress – or lack of it – of indentured apprentices. The court despatched James Knight, apprenticed to William Bragg, butcher, a 'notorious idle rogue' with a propensity for arson, to mend his ways in Exeter's House of Correction.

On 29 September 1685, William Terdrew of Northam, carpenter, who created a disturbance by attempting to break down Moses Langdon's door, was sentenced to be put in the High Street stocks for six hours, and afterwards to be bound over to appear before the General Sessions.

While Mr. and Mrs. William Joans attended matins service at Northam parish church on 21 July 1681, their home was broken into and a quantity of money and clothing stolen. Mr. Joans gave the village constable, John Leach, an inventory of missing items which included a straked (striped) handkerchief and a sad[4] coloured suit. Leach instituted a 'hue and cry', and it was not long before a stranger to the village, wearing a waistcoat similar in description to the stolen garment, came to his attention. The man gave his name as John Trehearne, a mariner of Pennar, Wales. On being arrested and searched, the Constable found £10 6s. 6¾d., a brass shilling and a striped handkerchief. Trehearne explained the money was back pay, and he had bought the handkerchief when in Jamaica. He claimed he had come to Bideford to visit his sisters and repay a loan from an old shipmate. He was unable to give the addresses of either his sisters or his shipmate. Dissatisfied with his story, Leach arrested Trehearne, charging him with theft, a capital offence. Bideford magistrates remanded him for trial before Exeter Assizes where he was found guilty and hanged.

Notwithstanding the poverty and deprivation of the ordinary townspeople, the majority remained honest in their dealings with each other. A Hartland woman, Jane Barnes, daughter of John Barnes of Milford, and servant to Henry Peryn, mariner, of Bideford, had good cause to be grateful for that honesty when a purse she had lost shortly before the Christmas of 1672 was returned to her with its contents, which included eight groats and a set of three false teeth, intact.

What of the fortunes of Bidefordians who had emigrated to the North American colonies? Here is the story of John Parker, who served as master-mate aboard the Pilgrim Fathers' – and Mothers' – ship, the *Mayflower*, on her historic voyage from Plymouth to the New World in 1620. Blown off course, the *Mayflower* made landfall on the.Massachusetts coast.

Fig. 12. Parker's Neck, Saco River, Canada. An impression of John Parker's trading post taken from an original print by James Patterson.

Parker founded a thriving fishing settlement at Parker's Island on the Saco River. Returning to England, he married Mary, who bore him three children, Thomas, John and Mary. Eventually the Parker family returned to America where John, senior, died in the 1660s. He bequeathed his estate to be divided among his children 'according to his wife's discretion'. John Parker II sold up his inheritance and moved westwards where he leased territory from a Sagamore Indian chieftain, nicknamed Robin Hood, for the price of:

one beaver skin, the quarterly rent of one bushel of corn and a quart of liquor to be paid unto Robin Hood or his heirs forever at or before 25 December yearly at the dwelling house of the said Parker reserving to himself and his heirs the right to fish, fowl, and hunt; also to set traps without molestation.

Before the white man decimated them by bullet and starvation, the Indians went on the warpath in a last attempt to win back their lost hunting grounds. In 1689, a war party razed John Parker's settlement to the ground. Parker and his son escaped the subsequent massacre by taking to the river and rowing to an army fort. Parker's Island became known by its present name, that of Biddeford in the state of Maine.

Disaster befell other settlers when a French army supported by Indian allies attacked and captured St John's, Newfoundland. In Bideford, townspeople who had business interests in the Colony suffered an estimated loss of over £24,000 while the settlers lost £12,000 – huge sums in those days.

In Europe, the war with France did not go well for England. An English and Dutch fleet commanded by Lord Torrington, Lord of the Manor of Torrington, engaged a French fleet off Beachy Head. Neither side fought with much commitment. The French claimed victory, having sunk or driven ashore four Dutch and one English men-o-war without loss to themselves.

The Admiralty recognised Bideford's maritime importance by giving its name to a 225-ton six-rater armed with 24 cannon and with 110 crew. *H.M.S. Bideford* was launched at Harwich in 1695. She was to be the first of a long line of naval vessels bearing the town's name. Her service was short, and she was wrecked in the West Indies four years after launching.

In the early years of the 18th century, Robert Harley (1661-1724), Speaker of the House of Commons, commissioned agents to report on the state of the country. Probably the most famous of his spies, Daniel Defoe, author of *Robinson Crusoe*, left a contemporaneous account of Bideford:

> Bideford is a pleasant, clean, well built town; the more ancient street which lies next the river, is very pleasant, where is the bridge, a very noble quay, and the custom house; this part also is very well built and populous, and fronts the river for above three quarters of a mile; but besides this, there is a spacious street [Bridgeland Street] broad as the High Street of Exeter, well-built, and which is more than all, well inhabited, with considerable and wealthy merchants, who trade to most parts of the trading world . . .
>
> The trade of this town being very much in fish, as it is also of all the towns on this coast, I observed here, that several ships were employed to go to Liverpool, and up the River Mersey to Warrington, to fetch rock salt, which is found in that county, which rock salt they bring to Bideford . . . to cure herrings . . .
>
> There is indeed, a very fine stone bridge over the river here, but the passage is so narrow, and they are so chary of it, that few carriages go over it; but as the water ebbs quite out of the river every low water, the carts and waggons go over the sand with great ease and safety; the arches of the bridge are beautiful and stately; but as for saying one of them is so big, that a ship of 60 tons may sail under it, as a late author asserts, I leave that where I find it, for the people of Bideford to laugh at.

But even as Defoe wrote his report, Bideford's deep sea fishing trade had begun to decline, crippled by a combination of war, piracy and American competition. By mid-century, the town's shipmasters had to content themselves by becoming middlemen, buying and transporting home from America cargoes of fish they had once trawled for so successfully. As the fishing trade contracted, so Torridgeside shipbuilding expanded. The first ship to have been built and registered in Bideford in the 18th century was the 50-ton *Diligence*, built in 1725. Between 1725 and the end of the century at least 186 vessels of varying tonnages were launched, the largest being a barquentine of 200 tons.

In the 18th century, Bideford imported more American tobacco than any other English port with the exception of London. Then, as now, tobacco carried a high excise duty. The huge profits gained by the evasion of the duty by diverting tobacco to Europe concentrated the minds of the unscrupulous. Such an entrepreneur was Thomas Benson, of Knapp House, Northam.

Born in 1707, Thomas was the third child of John Benson, a highly respected Northam merchant. In 1743, Thomas inherited the family firm and £40,000. Ignoring advice to diversify out of shipping, he wangled privateering licences out of his influential political friends, Lord Carteret, Secretary of State, and Lord Gower, Lord Privy Seal.

Captain Richard Vernan commanded the Benson privateer, *Benson Galley*, during 1743-4. Among the crew of 180 was James Bather who was to play a key role in Benson's downfall. Vernan later commanded the *Britania* which outfought an armed Spanish merchantman, killing or wounding 84 out of a crew of one hundred. In another adventure, he captured nine French fishing vessels worth £10,000. On a later voyage in the *Benson Galley* Vernan was forced to surrender to two 300-ton French men-o-war.

Another Benson ship, the *Newkey*, Captain Ley, with 13 guns, carrying 71 Irish passengers and 15 French prisoners-of-war, encountered the French privateer *Pierre et Marie* of Morlaix. Coming alongside the *Newkey* a French boarding party stormed aboard the English ship. After a desperate fight and with his shoulder shattered by a musket bullet, Ley struck his colours. The French captain, Lacoast, himself wounded and with eight of his men dead and another 10 wounded, treated his captives well 'because they were brave fellows'. The surviving Irish who had refused to fight were put in a longboat to row to the nearby Irish coast while Lacoast set sail for Brittany. But he made a terrible hash of his navigation by steering the *Pierre et Marie* between Lundy and Hartland in the belief that the mainland was that of France. When he realised his mistake, Lacoast surrendered to Ley who sailed his prize back to Bideford.

Although his privateering business had suffered serious setbacks, Benson came bouncing back. After an election which plumbed the depths of corruption he was returned to Parliament as M.P. for Barnstaple. At Westminster, he secured a lucrative contract to transport convicts to the colonies. He also obtained a lease on Lundy Island which was to be the centrepiece of a future he had planned for his unfortunate convict cargoes. During the century, a steady flow of men, women and child felons were sentenced to transportation often for the most trivial of crimes. For example, Charles Chesley of Buckland Brewer was sentenced to seven years' transportation for stealing 6lbs. of lamb, valued at 2s.0d. The Bideford court appointed John Ford and John Blinch to contract for Chesley's passage to America. The contract, worth £20, became void if Chesley died on the voyage or was captured by the enemy.

With an arrogance bordering on stupidity, Benson took Sir Thomas Gunson and a party of friends on a conducted tour of Lundy. What they saw amazed them. They watched convicts, who should have been in Virginia, building walls and excavating a deep cavern in the cliffs to store contraband goods. Without a trace of guilt, Benson boasted that he saw no difference between landing convicts on the island to slave for him instead of transporting the wretches across the Atlantic at great expense. 'It matters not where it was so long they were out of the country', he explained.

At the same time as Sir Thomas Gunson and his party digested Benson's crookedness, a Benson barque, the *Nightingale*, waited for custom's clearance at Appledore. Benson had planned a shameful end for the old ship. The 100-ton *Nightingale* had been at sea for half a century and her timbers were worm-eaten, her canvas rotten and her sheets perished. The old *Nightingale* was a coffin brig fit only for the insurance fraud Benson planned to execute. John Lancey, her master, was deeply involved in the conspiracy as was the bo'sun, James Bather, who had sailed in the *Britania*. Thomas Powe, an Appledore chandler, also played a crucial part in the swindle.

When the cargo had been stowed, the Collector of Customs went aboard with the bill of lading for Lancey's signature. The manifest included 365 bushels of salt and bales of kersey. Once the formalities had been completed the human flotsam from Exeter prison came aboard. A dozen men and three women, all in irons, were herded

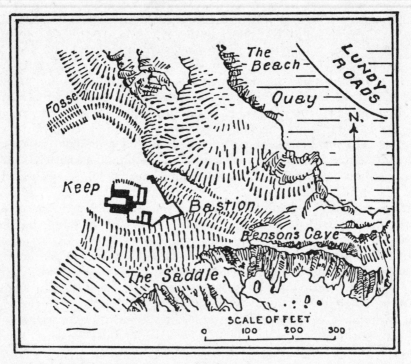

Fig. 13 Lundy Island, showing Thomas Benson's cave for hiding
contraband goods.

below to a platform rigged over the cargo hold. Before sailing, Ann Soar, 'a useful
woman and one that understands to make rabbit nets', arrived as a passenger for service
on Lundy. Young John Sinnett also joined the *Nightingale* as the ship's cook. He had
left a newly-wed wife behind. This was to be his first experience at sea.

From the grounds of Knapp House, Thomas Benson watched the *Nightingale* sail over
the Bar. After an eventful crossing, Lancey dropped anchor in a secluded quarter of
Lundy Roads. When Ann Soar had gone ashore, Lancey assembled his fellow conspirators for the pay-out. Lancey had already settled for £60. Lloyd, the mate, got £60;
James Bather refused to accept the £45 he had previously agreed to and demanded and
got an extra £5. Once the payments had been settled, the preparations for the faked
accident to destroy the *Nightingale* and her 'cargo' began. Concealing their activities
from the convicts, the conspirators offloaded the cargo with the exception of the water
barrels and salt. When the work had been completed, the *Nightingale* slipped her
moorings and got under way.

By 3 August, the *Nightingale* had sailed 50 miles west of Lundy. Here Lancey
exchanged signals with Captain Nicholson of the *Charming Nancy*. The sea was calm,
the visibility hazy. With the *Charming Nancy* close by to affect a rescue, but far enough
away not to witness the true fate of the *Nightingale*, Lancey ordered the destruction of
his ship. Sinnett went below to break open a smuggler's barrel hidden among the water
barrels. The secret compartments had been packed with highly inflammable bundles
of oakum impregnated with pitch which he positioned about the hold. Then he began
to chop a hole through the bulkhead separating the hold from the breadlocker. Bather

. The Longbridge before it was widened in 1864. Four adjacent quayside public houses, the *Steam Packet & Railway Hotel*, the *Newfoundland (Rose of Torridge)*, the *King's Arms* and the *Three Tuns Inn*, can be seen.

2. Bideford Quay in the 1880s. An 'Armada' gun barrel used as a mooring bollard stands to the left of the lamp-post.

3. The Longbridge, *c.* 1890. Stone parapets have been replaced by Victorian ironwork.

4. (*above*) Bideford Quay in the 1880s, showing the unmade road.

5. (*below*) The Quay and Bridgeland Street before 1896. The dark building on the right occupies the site of Bideford Art and Technical School. The three-storey block in the foreground was demolished in the post-World War II slum clearances.

Bideford Quay in the early 1900s before the arrival of the railway. The castellated riverside building is a public lavatory.

Bideford Quay in 1905 shortly after it had been widened. Trees have not yet been planted and the road is badly rutted.

8. A hunt meet at East-the-Water in the 1930s, near the statue of Sir Richard Pine Coffin. The ornate gas lamps which previously illuminated the Longbridge have been replaced by neon standards.

9. The Longbridge in 1924-5 when it was being widened. The ship at the Quay is probably a collier.

10.   Loading china clay in August 1984. The crane operator is Bob Westcott.

11.   Unloading fertiliser in August 1984.

12. The Quay in March 1984. Of the original 19th-century quayside inns, only the *King's Arms* and the *Talbot*—Bideford's 'Number One'—are still in business.

13. Day breaks over the Quay, August 1984.

14. (*below*) The Quay and Bridgeland Street in March 1984. The white building with flag flying was the Customs House, but is now a wine bar.

15.　The arrival of a L.S.W.R. holiday express at Bideford station.

16. A train at the bottom of Bridgeland Street, fitted with American-style 'cow-catcher' and wheel-shields to safeguard pedestrians. Note the single-engine buffer, a feature of B.W.Ho!A.R.'s three locomotives.

17. A L.S.W.R. excursion train arriving at Bideford mainline station, East-the-Water.

18. Bideford, Westward Ho! & Appledore Railway booking office and waiting room on Bideford Quay. The office now houses Peter Adams, Estate Agent.

19. The poorly cobbled road and pavement of Honestone Street in the 1890s.

20. Allhalland Street. The town's smallest shop with an eight feet frontage. The shop, which sold ice-cream in the 1930s, stands next to Torridgeside Planning Offices.

21.   Cross Street, Northam. Probably a First World War recruiting drive. An officer can be identified in the road at the centre of the middleground, and a soldier stands on the pavement beside the rear lorry.

22.   Bridgeland Street. The frontage of the 'Red House' is probably the finest example of 'mathematical' tiling in North Devon.

23. The corner of Mill Street and Willet Street c.1900, with the twin towers of Lavington church in the background.

24. The junction of the Quay and Bridge Street. The chemist shop beside the castellated guildhall is now the Council Chamber and Library.

25. Charles Kingsley is reputed to have written part of *Westward Ho!* in this room in the *Royal Hotel*, East-the-Water.

26. The old toll house at Potter's Corner, Torrington Lane, East-the-Water.

27. Bideford from Chudleigh's Fort, East-the-Water, in July 1984.

28. Ethelwynne Brown Close, East-the-Water, July 1984.

29. The Council Chambers and Library, August 1984.

30. (*left*) A fireplace dated 1623 which was exposed during renovations at Messrs. Chope's in the High Street, Bideford.

31. (*above*) Lower Meddon Street and the Quay. Once a part of the main route to the West.

32. (*below left*) 'Armada' guns in Victoria Park, March 1984.

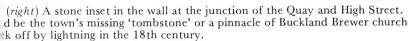

(*right*) A stone inset in the wall at the junction of the Quay and High Street.
d be the town's missing 'tombstone' or a pinnacle of Buckland Brewer church
k off by lightning in the 18th century.

34. (*left*) A portrait of Sir Richard Grenville by an unknown artist in 1571.

35. (*below left*) Charles Kingsley statue on Bideford Quay.

36. (*below*) John Richard Pine Coffin J.P. (1842-90). The bust stands on the probable site of a chapel which sold indulgences for the bridge's repair.

had to finish the job when Sinnett gashed his leg. After igniting the oakum, Bather axed through the rotten keel timbers, letting water flood in.

As smoke billowed from the hold, Lancey screamed at the convicts, accusing them of starting the fire. The terrified prisoners protested their innocence, pleading to be released before they were burnt alive. Theatrically, Lancey herded them aboard the longboat where they watched Bather and other members of the crew going through the motions of trying to put out the flames.

The fire aboard the *Nightingale* had been spotted by Captain Nicholson of the *Charming Nancy* who altered course to render assistance. Coming alongside the *Nightingale*, he rescued the convicts and the crew of the doomed ship. Nicholson had no reason to suspect that the fire was anything but an unfortunate accident. Later Nicholson transferred the 'shipwrecked men' to the brigantine *Endevour*, which took them into Clovelly.

Benson must have congratulated himself for pulling off the perfect crime. His insurers would never question the validity of a claim presented by a respected client like himself. However, a lifetime of unscrupulous dealings had earned him many bitter enemies, one of whom, Matthew Reeder, a Barnstaple merchant, overheard a drunken Lancey boasting to all and sundry of his role in the fraud. Reeder informed Benson's insurers who moved quickly. Lancey was arrested in the *Swan* alehouse in Northam and charged with fraud. Lloyd, Sinnett and Powe followed him into custody while Benson remained free.

Eighteen months after their arrest, the three men appeared before the Court of Admiralty at the Old Bailey. The charges against Sinnett were withdrawn. Lancey and Lloyd were accused of the capital offence of burning the *Nightingale* and being party to an attempt to defraud the insurers. The trial lasted seven hours. Found guilty, Lancey was sentenced to death, Powe was acquitted but retained in custody to stand trial at Exeter for other offences. Expelled from Parliament, Benson fled the country to avoid arrest. On 30 May, Lancey was conveyed to Execution Dock, Wapping, for public hanging. On the scaffold, he behaved 'very penitently', protesting his innocence to the last.

Powe remained in custody until 1758. James Bather published his version of the scandal, while Lloyd and Sinnett vanished into obscurity. Thomas Benson, the instigator of the whole scheme, died in Oporto at the age of 64. Besides his smuggler's cavern on Lundy Island, Benson's New Quay Dock, Appledore remains as a permanent reminder of the *Nightingale* scandal. His estate at Knapp House is now a holiday complex.

In the middle of the century, Bideford played reluctant host to a large French prisoner-of-war compound. A local observer highlighted the gulf in the conditions between ordinary prisoners and their officers:

Aug. 29, 1759. The town is at present made very brilliant by one half of the Somerset Militia who are sent to guard the French prison as needs require; there are about 1,000 poor fellows confined in a very close place without any hope of being sent home till Peace is concluded – none having ever yet been exchanged from hence, which makes them sometimes desperate. The officers are almost persons of large property and great distinction; and they have, most of them, their wives and families with them, at private lodgings, where they are pretty well accommodated, and give 2 guineas or two and a half guineas for them . . .

In stark contrast to the luxury and freedom in which officer prisoners lived, ordinary French soldiers were cooped up in a squalid, pestiferous camp bounded on the south and west by the Pill stream, and on the east by the Torridge. The half-starved, diseased inmates seethed with discontent at their conditions. Their anger burst into violence in October 1758, when they attempted a mass breakout. Guards shot dead one prisoner and grievously wounded many more. As a consequence of the riot, the prisoners were removed to a secure compound in the vicinity of Nutaberry, East-the-Water. The conditions in the camp were appalling. Admiralty officials who inspected the compound stated that the cubic footage allowed to each prisoner was totally inadequate, but nothing was done to rectify the situation.

Sailor prisoners whiled away their long days of boredom by modelling from bones superb replicas of the ships in which they had served. The completed models were bartered for food, tobacco or better living conditions. Some prisoners sold their work for a pittance. Examples of the P.O.W.s' modelling skill can be seen in Bideford's Burton Art Gallery which ironically stands close to the site of the Pillmouth P.O.W. camp.

The filthiness of the prison camp multiplied an already acute health hazard in the town. Recurrent epidemics raged through the overcrowded hovels of the poor. Their drinking water, taken from an excrement-polluted river or wells, carried the deadly bacilli of cholera, typhus, dysentery and other enteric sicknesses. A particularly severe epidemic of smallpox hit the town in 1719.

The townspeople did little to keep the streets clean. John Durant, a tallow chandler, and Thomas Harris (1723) were arraigned for having left a dead cow for several days in a house in Old Town, 'and it was proper stinking'. John Moyse was held responsible for permitting dung to be heaped on the quay and later in Buttgarden Street. The churchwardens were reprimanded for having a dung heap inside the churchyard. The council appointed Samuel Matthews and William Hobbs (1757) to indicate the proper places for dung heaps and to supervise their removal. The town scavengers were presented in 1765 for failing to clean the market and leaving dung heaps in several parts of the town.

As the century progressed, so medical knowledge improved. A growing understanding of the relationship of insanitary living conditions to disease caused the council to insist that people must improve drainage in the lanes and streets. In 1788, the inhabitants of Honestone Street, High Street and New Street to the end of Potter's Lane (North Road) were urged to provide a proper water gutter for the safety of travellers and horse passengers.

The religious affairs of mid-18th-century Bideford were dominated by the long incumbency of the Reverend John Whitfield, Professor of Poetry, as vicar of St Mary's, a divine of a contentious nature. Whitfield had little respect for many of the town's influential parishioners and even less for its officials. Summoned for non-payment of parish dues, he gathered together all council documents referring to the church and scattered them over the chancel floor, challenging the council to 'remove this rubbish, for I will have them no longer in my church'. But he nullified his demonstration by locking up the church. He outraged his parishioners by refusing to bury a baby whose corpse rotted by the altar for several weeks before a High Court writ forced him to relent. During the period of the closure of the church, the Guildhall was used for divine service. A bell cast to summon the faithful to prayer had inscribed around the rim the epigram: 'Our Parson's pride formed a bell. By that I rose. By that Satan fell'. After Whitfield condescended to open the church, his extraordinary behaviour gave so much offence that the council complained to the Bishop of Exeter. They instanced an occasion when Whitfield offered a prayer beseeching the Almighty to deliver him from the scum of mankind, 'this scoundres people'. He then spat on Mayor George Buck, swearing that the Buck family was a gang of scoundrels. He followed this up by grabbing the mayor by the collar and kicking him on the shins. When the town clerk intervened, Whitfield punched him in the face. The parishioners were very upset by the altercation, 'some wept, others fainted, and the whole congregation was put into the utmost confusion and distraction'. Remarkably, Whitfield's 41-year incumbency at St Mary's (1742-83) was the longest in the parish's history.

An 18th-century Bideford-born eccentric noted for his peculiar demeanour and lifestyle was the gentle Thomas Stuckley (1681-c.1738), son of the Reverend Lewis Stuckley, one-time chaplain to Oliver Cromwell, who had taken up residence in Bridgeland Street[5] after his expulsion from Exeter Cathedral for his contentious principles. As a young man, Thomas read law at London's Middle Temple. On his father's death, he returned to Bridgeland Street. He gave up law to devote his life to solving such problems as the quadrature of the circle and perpetual motion. He became a recluse and a hypochondriac, haunted by fears of succumbing to fever or dying from neglect. Yet he chose to live in squalor. He rarely claimed monies owing to him. When he received payment in coinage, he disinfected them in a bucket of water.

Thomas's peculiar lifestyle excited the inquisitiveness of the townspeople. When he had to leave his house to swear allegiance to George I, a crowd gathered to watch him emerge into daylight for the first time for years. He wore a little round tarred hat plonked on an unruly mop of hair, with a dishevelled beard straggling over his chest. His clothes were little more than rags for he eschewed new garments for fear the material carried disease. After his public appearance, Thomas returned to his house and shut the door behind him. With the exception of his servants, whom he treated well, he remained behind closed doors until his death.

Besides his mathematical studies, Thomas interested himself in current affairs, especially with the Duke of Marlborough's campaign in the Low Countries. He followed the strategy of the Duke's battles by gouging battle maps in the kitchen floor, which was made in the Devon fashion of ash and lime compounded together. Each battle cost him the laying of a new floor. Thomas, in his perambulations, wore deep furrows in the bedroom floor on each side of which gold and silver coins were scattered. In the kitchen, he had dug a pit before the cooking fire in which he sat to keep warm. Thomas died c. 1737. Washed clean of filth and lice, his body was interred in the family vault at West Worlingham, near Winkleigh.

A contemporary of Thomas Stuckley, John Shebbeare, political firebrand and scourge of the establishment, was born in Bideford shortly after his father, Richard, attorney-at-law, and his wife moved from Shebbeare Town,[6] Northam to Bideford to be closer to his law practice. After being educated by Mr. Zachary Mudge at Bideford Grammar School, John was apprenticed to John Marks, surgeon and apothecary. After gaining his indentures, he married a Miss Cornish and set up in business on his own account. Ambition drove him to quit Bideford and seek fame and fortune in Bristol where he went into partnership with an established apothecary. In 1740, he published a paper praising the efficacy of the city's spa of Hotwells.

During 1734, John published *The Marriage Act*, a novel in which he lampooned the Whig administration. He was arrested and kept in custody for a short time. Undeterred, he continued his vendetta against the government. On the publication of the third in a scries of 'Letters to the People of England', he was re-arrested and charged with sedition. This time he was fined heavily, given a three-year prison stretch and sentenced to be pilloried.

John escaped the humiliation and pain of a pilloring because an old school chum of his, Mr. Beardmore, Under-Sheriff of London, permitted his friend to stand beside the Charing Cross pillory while a footman held an umbrella over his head to ward off the rain and the odd missile. For his leniency, Beardmore was sacked, fined £50 and sentenced to two months' imprisonment.

Having served his sentence in full, Shebbeare was released, broken in health and spirit. Realising that a further term in jail would probably kill him, he made his peace with the Whigs, accepting an annual £200 pension from the Prime Minister. To the disgust of his many admirers Shebbeare seemed to have become the stooge of the political party he had attacked with such venom, but in private, he stuck to his anti-Whig principles. He died in London on 1 August 1788.

Unlike the seditious John Shebbeare, Benjamin Donne (1729-98) never antagonised the state. He did, however, have scholastic disagreements with fellow academicians. The Donne family had lived in Bideford for three generations before George Donne entered the pages of the town's history. In the early 18th century, George opened a school in Allhalland Street close to Zachary Mudge's Grammar School. While the latter concentrated on the classics, George taught navigation, astronomy, ship design and commercial book-keeping. A pillar of the community, George acted as parish clerk for a quarter of a century from June 1721. He was empowered to collect 4d. annually from every family in the parish as a means to pay his salary.

Born in 1729, George's son, Benjamin, showed an aptitude for mathematics and became an expert in the contemporary science of natural and experimental philosophy. When his father's survey of the Longbridge appeared in the *Gentleman's Magazine* it was accompanied by an article written by Benjamin. In further contributions to the magazine, Benjamin gave detailed accounts of solar and lunar eclipses he had witnessed in Bideford.

For several years he taught at the family school specialising in mathematics and Newtonian theories, before moving to Bristol to take up the appointment of City Librarian. He fell out with the City Fathers by proposing that the educational curriculum of the library should be extended to include mathematics. The dispute led to his resignation. He opened a commercial academy in the city, publishing his *Young Shopkeeper's and etc., Companion* as a basic textbook for his pupils. He also found time to deliver lectures on philosophy.

His enduring claim to national fame was as a cartographer. He won a £100 prize from the Society of Arts for producing expertly surveyed maps of Devon and its principle cities. He followed up his success with a detailed map of Bristol and a pocket map of the city. Besides Devon, he mapped Hampshire, Dorset, Somerset and Cornwall as well as designing mathematical instruments. In 1789, he published *Mathematical Tables*. Shortly before his death, George III appointed him as his 'Master of Mechanics' in recognition of his services to mathematics and cartography.

Judicial cruelty co-existed with cultural enlightenment. While the Donnes and Zachary Mudge instilled knowledge into their pupils in Allhalland Street, male and female felons were flogged by the school windows. The first recorded whipping of a woman in Bideford occurred in 1716 when Mary Owen was sentenced to be stripped to

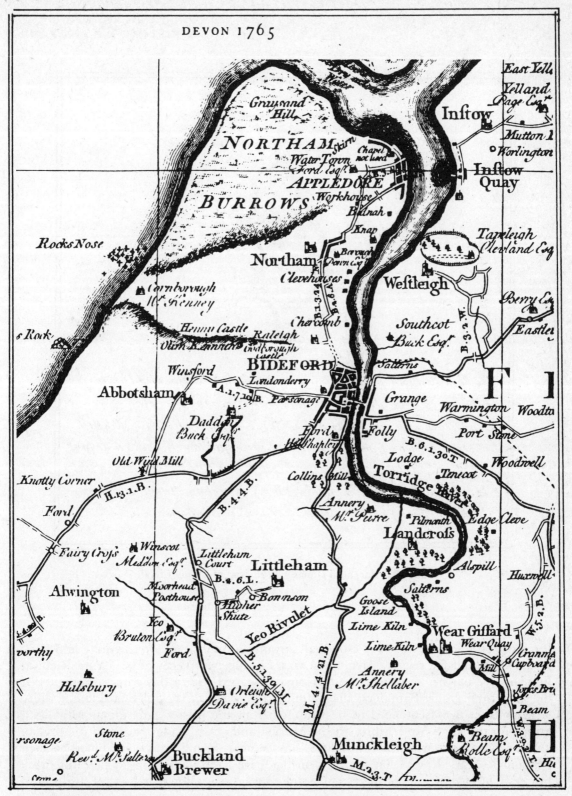

Fig. 14. Benjamin Donne's 1765 Map of Bideford/Northam. Kenwith Castle is indicated as Henny Castle.

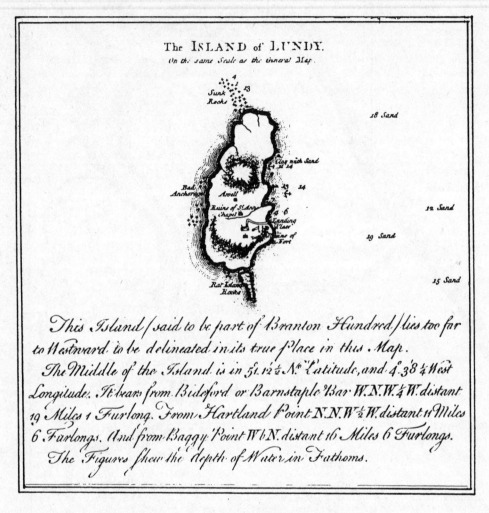

Fig. 15. Benjamin Donne's 1765 Map of Lundy Island.

the waist and flogged from the Guildhall, around a tombstone[7] on the quay and back to the Guildhall for release. Her crime was stealing two pieces of beef from Richard French. Her partner in crime, Henry Comer, escaped with a day's imprisonment. At the same time, James Saunders, alias Vinney, a labourer of Weare Giffard found guilty of petty theft, was sentenced to be whipped from the prison gate, along Allhalland Street, up the High Street, through the Market and down Bridge Street to the prison. The magistrate exhorted the whipman to 'lay on heartily and bring some blood by such whipping'. Mary Rogers felt the lash on her bare back for stealing a piece of black brick valued at 10d., the property of George Strang, a wealthy merchant of Bridgeland Street.

In 1767, the town council expressed its alarm that a gang of ruffians were terrorising the town. Vigilante patrols were formed to assist the constables in policing the streets.

Besides this outbreak of lawlessness, the magistrates had the usual crop of petty misdemeanours to control, including that of bull-baiting at a ring in Bull Hill. To the risk of life and limb of the populace, savage bulldogs had joined the ubiquitous pigs roaming the town. A summons against Hezekiah Hunt for allowing his dogs to run about the streets was withdrawn when the animals were destroyed. The incorrigible Hezekiah soon acquired another bulldog, 'a very dangerous animal', which again brought him before the court. This time he was severely reprimanded. During 1769, Hezekiah found himself in the dock once again, this time for managing a cockpit outside his house. John Futts was found guilty of keeping a ninepin skittle alley which 'tended to the encouragment of idleness and gaming'. The charge aginst Mary Passmore (1791) for having a billiard table was dismissed. John Biggs of Barnstaple (1794) applied successfully for a licence to perform drama and other theatrical entertainment in the Borough for not more than 60 days between 7 January and 17 March.

The civic life of the Borough ended the century with the granting of the Freedom of the Town to Colonel the Right Honourable Lord John Rolle and the officers of the South Devon Regiment in a colourful ceremony for rendering 'essential service in suppressing Wolfe Tone's rebellion in Ireland'.

An earlier rebellion against the British, the American War of Independence (1775-81), undermined Bideford's position as a leading tobacco port. Ironically, it was an American official of Bideford descent who played a crucial part in the collapse of the trade which had brought such wealth to the town. At Boston, Massachusetts, Nathaniel Coffin, King's Cashier of Customs, whose forebear Tristram Coffin of Alwington had emigrated to America in the 1640s, enforced the collection of Stamp Duty on certain imports. The tax enraged the settlers and led to the Boston Tea Party incident and armed rebellion. After the war the bulk of American tobacco imports were landed at Bristol and London.

The American conflict coupled with the seemingly endless wars with the French gave rise to several epic sea battles involving West Countrymen. It was a David versus Goliath engagement between the Royal Naval frigates, *H.M.S. Biddeford* and the *Flamborough* and two heavier and better armed French frigates that electrified Torridge-side.

Launched at Deptford, London, in the 1750s, the *Biddeford* was the fourth naval ship to bear the town's name. A sixth rater, she mounted 20 cannon, weighed 450 tons and carried 160 crew. On 4 April 1760 the *Biddeford*, Captain Lancelot Skynner, and the *Flamborough*, Captain Archibald Kennedy, were on station near the Lisbon Rock ready to give protection to an allied convoy. During the afternoon, the *Flamborough* sighted the enemy frigates, *L'Omphiale* and *La Maliceuse*, approaching. The two English captains 'murdered no time' in deciding to engage the enemy, a resolution which 'staggered the French'. While the *Flamborough* opened fire on *L'Omphiale*, the *Biddeford* set about *La Maliceuse*, flying the ensign of the flotilla commander. In the ensuing battle a cannon ball killed Captain Skynner. Despite his death and the wounding of the First Officer, Mr. Knollis, *Biddeford*'s gunners drove off the Frenchmen. The *Flamborough* sustained five dead and 10 wounded. Three days after the battle, the *Biddeford* limped into Lisbon and shortly after docking, Knollis died from his wounds. Both men were buried in Lisbon with full naval honours.

Another war hero with direct family ties with Bideford, Captain George Farmer, commanded the frigate *H.M.S. Quebec* when she fought the greatly superior enemy frigate, *La Surveille* off Ushant in 1799:

> The contest on both sides was desperate, and Capt. Farmer displayed such gallantry and intrepidity that he continued the engagement until his own ship, accidentally taking fire, was blown into the air. When last seen, Farmer was . . . sitting on the anchor fluke.

Captain Farmer's grandson became foreman of the Bideford jury. The fifth and last of the line, a baronet, who lived in Buckland Brewer, worked as a ropemaker in Bideford and died in reduced circumstances in 1913.

To be shipwrecked in Bideford Bay – as elsewhere – in the 18th century was fraught with danger. Not only had the victims to contend with the fury of the elements but also with the mobs of looters attracted by the pickings. They would strip the wreck of everything of value, and were not averse to slitting the throats of anyone who stood in their way. The *Gentleman's Magazine* of February 1790 carried an account of the fate of the French merchantman, *La Carpe*:

> On Wednesday last, *La Carpe*, was drove ashore between this place [Bideford] and Abbotsham, a French 20-gun ship of about 400 tons, Michel Burel, commander, laden with timber, oil and wine. Captain Burel with 35 hands are saved, and 14 are drowned. As soon as they set foot ashore, the country people to the number of 2,000 boarded the ship with hooks, hatchets, and other instruments, and immediately began to plunder, and cut down all the rigging, sails, masts, and yards; the cabins they broke up, and carried off all the Captain's boxes, chests, laced clothes, swords with some silk and linens, 1,400 quintals of cod, many barrels of herrings, and in short everything they could lay their hands on. The cables and rigging they cut into junk, and carried it off in waggons and horses. They also drank out all the wine on being five hogsheads. The Customs-House officers that were sent to protect and save the ship and cargo, were in great danger of their lives, being threatened by these inhuman plunderers to be cut down with their hatchets, or thrown into the sea. One of them was surrounded by twenty of these barbarians for attempting to save a box out of the ship; and they would have drowned him had it not been for the interposition of one of our country gentlemen. These are the very same fellows who plundered and broke up the Dutch ship that was on shore about six months ago near the same place. We hear the Captain has applied to a merchant at Lyme, and that by his assistance he has procured warrants for apprehending a great many of those miscreants; and it is hoped that some of those miscreants will be brought to condign punishment, etc.

A memorial to Mary Golding, drowned in the loss of *H.M.S. Weazle*, exists in Northam churchyard. Outward bound from Appledore to Falmouth on 12 February 1799, the *Weazle* foundered on the Morte Rock in a violent storm. All 106 aboard were drowned. The reason why the young lady was aboard a naval ship can only be surmised.

By the end of the century, the appearance and condition of the town had deteriorated alarmingly. No longer was it Daniel Defoe's 'pleasant clean and well built town'. Instead Marshall, in his *Rural Economy of the West of England* published in 1794, describes Bideford:

> The Town is remarkably forbidding. Meanly built houses, (timber, brick, or mud, covered with bad slate or thatch), struck against a steep hill. The streets . . . are awkward; and most of them are narrow, in the vacant spaces between the streets immense piles of furze faggots, in the shape of houses, and make the houses appear more like hovels than they really are. The dangerous piles of fuel are for the use of the pottery for which only, I believe, this town is celebrated; chiefly or wholly, the coarser kinds of earthen ware.
>
> The tide is out; many men employed in loading packhorses with sand, left in the bed of the river. In every vacant corner about the town, [heaps] composing of earth, mud, ashes, etc., are seen. Shell sand is said to be plentiful on the coasts; but little, if any of it, is brought up their river.
>
> The Bridge of Bideford is an extraordinary erection; a high, thick wall, run across the river or narrowed estuary; with Gothic gateways, here and there, to let water pass.

On the shore of the estuary, opposite the town, are several limekilns, now in full work. Number of packhorses, and a few carts, loading or waiting for loads. The stone, chiefly, and the culm which it is burnt, wholly, brought across the channel, from the coast of Wales. The Kilns similar to those of West Devonshire. This lime is carried fourteen or fifteen miles chiefly on horseback . . .

Bideford held its main market on Tuesdays. Lesser markets were held on Saturdays, and in summer, on Thursdays as well. The market house was described as being commodious. All kinds of farm and garden produce were offered for sale. At the stroke of one o'clock, the market bell was rung for the sale of wheat to the public for one hour. No baker was allowed to buy in stock until two o'clock. By this method, coupled with a strict licensing system for corn dealers and bakers, the council strove to protect the poor from the unscrupulous who hoarded wheat to keep the price high. In the market, meat sold at from 4d. to 9d. per pound; a brace of hens or ducks cost from 9d. to 2s.0d.; a 4lb. loaf 'of the quality of soldiers' best bread' sold at about one shilling.

To protect the Longbridge, the Trustees encouraged clusters of giant mussels to adhere to the cuttwaters. Those found guilty of poaching these crustacea were liable to tranportation to a penal colony.

As the century drew to a close, Roger Chope, Charles Smith, Elizabeth Stavely and Thomas Stocker were summoned for enclosing and locking up the public water pump at the top of Bridge Street. The court ordered the defendants to re-open the facility, at the same time warning those users who refused to contribute to its maintenance that they could be denied access to the pump.

Chapter Five

THE NINETEENTH CENTURY

AT THE TURN of the century, press gangs scoured North Devon, seizing seamen for naval service against Napoleon Bonaparte's France. Seventeen-year-old Richard Hobbs, of Bideford, was among those taken. He served in the battleship, *Thunderer*, at the Battle of Trafalgar. Richard survived the war, dying in Bideford at the age of eighty-one. Midshipman Barton, whose family had inherited Burrough House, Northam, served aboard Nelson's *Victory* at Trafalgar. Before Napoleon's exile to the isle of St Helena, Major-General John Pine Coffin of Portledge had the defeated emperor in his custody.

On the home front, the council continued the struggle to improve the condition of the town. The Harbour Master (1801) found himself in trouble for allowing ships' bottoms to be burnt near the quay and for permitting pitch pots to be heated on their decks. The council also recommended to the court the necessity for adopting lawful pewter measures for the sale of ale and beer.

During 1807, the council cracked down on those who disturbed the Sabbath peace by:

> Viz, Skittle Alleys, and Cock Fighting at private houses; they likewise request that a stop may be put to the very improper and riotous conduct practised within the Town on Sunday evenings to the great annoyance of the inhabitants.

They appointed an official to issue summons to:

> . . . bring forward those people . . . who leave carts and etc, in different parts of the Town, particularly the Quay, where they are left to the great risk of passengers; also drivers for riding their carts without a guide for the horses.

Charles Hatherley was the first Bidefordian to have the dubious honour of collecting a 'parking ticket' for leaving his post-chaise unattended in the street.

Magistrates came down heavily on those found guilty of vandalism. For deliberately knocking down a wall on the newly opened Bideford-Torrington road (1827), John Wray was sentenced to two months' working the treadmill.

Despite the council's efforts to keep the town clean, the fly-tipping of litter and dung continued. Thomas Burnard (1807) was summoned for piling rubbish close to the theatre on the quay. Whipping remained as a penalty for those committing petty offences. Found guilty of stealing a printed calico gown and a coat from Thomas Samm, Sarah MacWiggin was publicly flogged from the *New Inn*, round the Market House and back to the *New Inn*. Richard Trick and William Taylor, who had been found guilty of stealing three pecks of barley, were whipped from the Guildhall, down the quay, up the High Street, through the market and back to the Guildhall.

The European war had spread across the Atlantic when the United States of America allied themselves with France. American privateers preyed on shipping in the Bristol Channel. *The Times* complained of the ravages meted out by the raiders:

> They daily enter in among our convoys, seize prizes in sight of those that should afford protection and if pursued, put on sea wings, and laugh at the clumsy English pursuers. To what is this owing? Cannot we build ships?

Torridgeside shipyards certainly did build ships of high quality. From 1786 to 1800, 157 vessels were launched, among the biggest being the *Fanny* of 228 tons. From 1800 to the end of the Napoleonic war (1815) approximately 200 vessels, including warships, came out of Torridgeside yards.

The early years of the century were not only stained by the tragedies of war but by the dramas of civil unrest. When the North Devon Agricultural Society (1812) introduced the standardised Winchester corn measure into Bideford market, many townspeople reckoned they were being cheated. So high did feelings run that a principal of the Society received an anonymous letter reflecting the people's anger:

> Winter nights is not long past therefore your person shall not go home alive – or if you chance to escape the hand that guides the pen, a lighted match will do execution. Your family, I know not, but the whole shall be enveloped in flames, your Carcase, if any such should be found, will be given to the Dogs if it contains any moisture for the animals to devour it.

In the famine year of 1816, a serious outbreak of civil unrest occurred in the town. On 23 May, the spectacle of farmers loading potatoes aboard a ship at the quay, to claim higher prices in up-country markets, triggered off a riot. The town clerk, Tom Salt, hurried to the quay where he met with some difficulties: 'It is stated the Town Clerk got upon a barrel to read the Riot Act, when shipbuilders knocked the top in, and rolled the official (who was but 4ft. in height) down the hill'.

The official report of what became known as the Bideford Potato Riot stated:

> In consequence of a cargo of potatoes being about to be shipped at the Quay of Bideford, a great number of people collected, armed with bludgeons and other weapons, to prevent the exportation taking place. The police of the town apprehended three of the ringleaders and confined them in the town prison. Immediately on the event being known, an immense number of shipwrights and others beat off the police, broke down the prison doors and released the prisoners. An express was sent off to the North Devon Yeomanry who promptly assembled; the riot was immediately dispersed. The cavalry remained under arms and patrolled the town during the night. On Saturday morning several of the rioters were apprehended and four of them sent to Exeter under an escort of the North Devon Yeomanry Cavalry. They are now in the County Prison.
>
> On information being given that a great number of disorderly people were collecting at Appledore and Cleave Houses, the cavalry proceeded to the latter to secure about 30-40 who were arming themselves with various weapons. When the troops appeared, the offenders went board a ship which was surrounded by the tide and lowering the boats, went off to the Braunton side of the water and made their escape. We are happy to say no lives have been lost. Too much praise cannot be bestowed on the North Devon Yeomanry for their behaviour in quelling the riot in its infancy. On Saturday night everything was perfectly tranquil. Soon after 40 Enniskillen Dragoons arrived and relieved the Yeomanry who had been on duty two nights.

So seriously did the government treat the riot, that the Home Secretary despatched Mr. Stafford and a squad of his Bow Street Runners[1] to Bideford with instructions to 'root out principal troublemakers not already in custody'. The Runners soon arrested another ringleader who was consigned to join his fellow riot leaders already under lock and key in Exeter's clink. On 15 August, the five stood trial, charged with riotous assembly. All were found guilty and sentenced to prison, Thomas Trace for two years, Thomas Crocombe for 18 months, William Moyrick, James Stapledon and George Veals for six months each.

A near riot occurred in the town on Midsummer Day 1838, when gatecrashers attempted to break up a teetotallers' meeting being held at the Guildhall:

> Several of the veterans of the [alcoholic] traffic, such as spirit dealers, publicans and doctors, with a host of others interested in the trade, whose minds were enveloped by the fumes of inebriation, attempted to take possession of the rooms by force and drive thence the teetotallers, but these intruders were gallantly repulsed and after several attempts to take the room, were finally worst'ed. They would have a good hiding, but the teetotallers had mercy upon them, and did not wish to take advantage of their drunken freaks, but held possession of their Citadel, as a mark of valour for the cause they espoused.
>
> The cause still went on vigorously and several efficient meetings were held in the vicinity; and at the anniversary held at Christmas, 1838, the Society and its branch membership numbered 507, 77 of these reclaimed drunkards, and 40 of them were united to Christian Churches.

After their drubbing at the Guildhall, the tippling fraternity had not many yards to go to drown their humiliation, for Bideford had 42 public houses and 28 ale houses.

If he was found guilty of causing a breach of the peace, a drunk might find himself picking oakum or breaking stones in the town's Meddon Street prison. Incorporated with the workhouse, the gaol consisted of six cells for ordinary prisoners and a separate 'apartment' for debtors. At a later date, wine cellars beneath the Colonial Building (now the *Royal Hotel*, East-the-Water) were utilised as prison cells. Nearby a battery of cages for lunatics were sited on what was to become Bideford's mainline railway station.

The following statistics have been extracted from the government census of 1833:

> The Borough of Bideford extends over 4,510 acres. At the last census it contained a population of 4,846*, comprising 995 familes who were chiefly engaged in trade, handicraft or industry; 105 were employed in agriculture. There were 990 inhabited houses . . .

Since 1801, the town's population had risen by over two-thirds.

On the northern side of the town, a ribbon development of expensive mansions connected Bideford with the village of Northam. Appledore had 381 dwellings almost exclusively inhabited by shipwrights, boatmen and mariners. Only 22 families earned enough to be taxed, the total amount collected being £63.

Bideford Corporation consisted of a mayor, eight aldermen and 10 capital burgesses. The borough officers were composed of a recorder, a town clerk, a coroner, two mace bearers, a chief constable, 16 constables, a beadle, a market clerk, two surveyors of weights and measures, a receiver of Assize returns, a gaoler, and a town crier. Voted in by the Corporation, the mayor took office on 21 September, and his appointment lasted for one year. As justice of the peace and chairman of the Assize court he received an allowance of £20 a year. An unsalaried recorder – 'a discreet man, skilled in the laws of England' – was elected in a similar manner to the mayor. A prospective town clerk had to be a 'worthy and discreet man'. His appointment was for life if he behaved himself. Elected annually, the coroner received the usual fees of office. The duties of the two sergeants-at-mace included the collection of fines and rents. Provided with hats and cloaks by the Corporation, they received £3 per annum. The mayor appointed 16

(* 1981 census: Bideford, 13,826; Appledore, 2,135; Northam, 4,743)

Fig. 16. *Royal Hotel*, East-the-Water. This was John Buck's town mansion and once the wine cellars were prison cells.

constables annually. The chief constable was paid three guineas per annum out of the parish rate. The Corporation appointed the head gaoler. As well as being paid £10 per .annum, he received a further £10 for being workhouse governor. A house went with the job. The beadle acted as town crier and attended the mayor at Assizes. The offices of market superintendent and surveyor of weights were within the mayor's patronage.

During May 1841, Thomas Lander, 56, and Thomas Willis, 24, tried unsuccessfully to spring 29-year-old Jane Willis from the town jail where she waited to be transported, her crime being that of stealing silk and calico from her employer, V. Vellacott. Both men were apprehended. After spending 48 hours in custody, the pair were released with no charges being preferred against them. Jane, probably the wife of Thomas Willis, was transported.

At the Epiphany Sessions 1845, the magistrates committed John Stoyle to a month's hard labour for the theft of a hat. At the Michaelmas Sessions, Bridget Harris was found guilty of stealing a silver watch and chain, two seals and a latchkey. For this, her second conviction, Bridget was sentenced to seven years' transportation. She was sent to Plymouth's Millbank Prison to await a berth aboard a prison hulk. The coroner received a fee of 2s.0d. for each indictment.

In the tightly-packed jumble of houses, many thatched and nearly all with bundles of tinder dry furze against the walls, the risk of a catastrophic fire was enormous. In 1795, funds became available for the town to purchase a fire engine. The *Bideford Gazette* of 15 December 1857 carried an account of a serious fire at tenant farmer Thomas Brayley's Southcott Farm, Westleigh. Immediately the fire was reported, Chief Firefighter William Major had the horses harnessed to the fire engine. With the furnace of the pump belching out sparks from the chimney, the firefighters set out for Westleigh. Another engine owned by the West of England Insurance Company followed close behind. By the time the two rigs had reached Barnstaple Street, a large crowd had joined the firefighters, for the spectacle of a good fire was not to be missed.

When the firemen reached the farm, all the buildings were blazing out of control. By dawn, Southcott Farm had been reduced to smouldering heaps of rubble. At the subsequent official enquiry, the coroner blamed a dairymaid for accidentally starting the conflagration by dropping a glowing lump of charcoal from a shovelful she was taking to the creamery to scald milk. Luckily for the landlord, Mr. L.W. Buck, his insurance policy covered such a disaster. Thomas Brayley and his workers were not so fortunate, 'loosing every vestige of their apparel'. They did not get a penny in compensation.

The years had long passed since Tom Faggus, riding his strawberry roan, had robbed travellers using the rutted tracks which had served as North Devon roads. Now, a well maintained and policed network of toll roads linked communities one with another. Those caught attempting to evade payment of the toll could expect to be dealt with severely. William Westcott was fined £5 with 14s.6d. costs for driving a horse and cart through Westcombe turnpike without paying the toll.

Regular coach services connected Bideford with Exeter, Torrington, Barnstaple and Plymouth. Since the opening of the New Road on the west bank of the Torridge (A.386), Torrington-bound traffic no longer had to toil up Torrington Lane, East-the-Water and negotiate the narrow, winding Gammaton-Huntshaw-Torrington road. The landlord of Bideford's *New Inn* is reputed to have bribed the road builders to divert the route of the New Road from the quay so that it linked with Buttgarden Street and his hotel. By this means he secured the monopoly of stagecoach traffic.

Road accidents in the days of horse-drawn traffic were not infrequent. As dusk fell on 16 February 1847, the Torrington-bound coach stood on the quay waiting to start the 6 p.m. journey. As St Mary's church clock struck the hour, Driver George Bowden cracked his whip over his horse and the coach rumbled on its way. All the inside seats had been occupied by Torrington folk. Mrs. Fanny Friendship, a widow of New Street, Torrington, travelled with her daughter, Elizabeth, and her 11-year-old granddaughter, Mary Ann. The other travellers were Michael Chappell, glovemaker, his brother John, fellmonger, and Thomas Passmore, worsted manufacturer. Outside an unnamed woman sat with Driver Bowden on the driving bench.

Hardly had the coach got under way when the horse took fright. Despite Bowden applying the brakes, the coach rolled backwards over the edge of the quay. Thrown into the freezing water, Bowden and the outside passenger were quickly hauled to safety. Michael Chappell managed to force a door open and escaped before the water pressure slammed it shut for good. Onlookers watched helplessly as the coach, with its doomed passengers trapped inside, drifted downstream with the tide, sinking lower and lower in the water until it finally disappeared. Not until low tide could the coach be dragged from the river bed. By then all the passengers had been dead for hours.

At the inquest, the coroner refuted allegations that Driver Bowden had been drunk at the time of the disaster and a verdict of 'accidental death' was returned on the unfortunate victims of the tragedy. A tombstone in Torrington cemetery marks the grave

Fig. 17. Bideford in the 1820s. At this time no direct road links existed to Torrington or Instow. Barnstaple traffic was routed along what is now the Old Barnstaple Road.

of Thomas Passmore. On the night of the disaster, a drunken Richard Prince fell into Clovelly harbour and was drowned.

After the end of the Napoleonic War, revolutionary technological change took place on the Torridge River as steam propulsion began to challenge and then supercede sail. During 1817, Irish-bound steamships established Ilfracombe as a summer terminal for a regular passenger service between Devon and Cork. At first, limited cargo space meant the steamers could not compete for freight traffic with the sturdy Bideford 'poluccas' trading out of the Torridge.

In July 1827 a short-lived passenger service linked Bideford with Barnstaple and

Bristol. Quick to appreciate the advantages of operating a passenger service not reliant on wind and tide, a North Devon and Bristol business consortium tendered for a steamship of 180-220 tons and a power capacity of 90-100 horsepower. William Clibbett's Richmond Yard, Appledore, won the contract. Launched in February 1835, the *Torridge*, the first steamship to be built on the Torridge, was schooner-rigged and carvel-hulled. She had a single deck and a standing bowsprit with a male figure beneath. Unfortunately, the *Torridge*'s propulsion unit was plagued with teething troubles, and her owners sold her to the Bristol Steam Navigation Company. Her new owners rectified the faults and the *Torridge* remained in service for 40 years.

Inaugurated in 1845, the North Devon Steamship Company filled the gap caused the by the sale of the *Torridge* by purchasing the 74-ton paddle-steamer *Water Witch*. She plied between Bideford and Bristol for 10 years.

An advertisement (1852) announced that the Bristol General Steamship Company would be operating the screw-driven *Princess Royal* on a weekly return trip between Bideford and Bristol, the fare being 9s.0d. for saloon passengers and 5s.0d. for forecastle cabins. For the next 15 years, she sailed the Bristol Channel before being sold. Another steamship which became a familiar sight at Bideford quay was the 98-ton *Neath Abbey*. She met her end on the rocks off Nash Point, South Wales, with the loss of four of her crew of seven. She was replaced by the *Marquess of Lorne* on the Bideford-Bristol run.

Arguably the best-loved of the Bideford steam packets was the *Devonia*. Owned and operated by the Bideford and Bristol Steamship Company, a non-profit making co-operative headed by Bideford grocer, Edward J. Tattersall, the *Devonia* had been built at the Irvine shipyard in Scotland. She measured 85 feet and weighed 95 tons, and was powered by a compound two-cylinder engine set aft. For 40 years, she was captained by Francis George Trowbridge of Bideford. A few days after his retirement in 1940, the *Devonia* struck a German sea mine near Cardiff whilst on passage to Ely. She sank almost immediately, the only survivor being William Turner of East-the-Water.

The advent of the Industrial Revolution, coupled with a spate of canal building, encouraged Lord Rolle of Stevenstone to privately finance the building of a waterway connecting Bideford with Torrington. He appointed John Green to survey and supervise his project. Green chose a route roughly following a course parallel to the Torridge, starting at Landcross, through Weare Giffard, Taddyport, Torrington and from there to its terminal at Healand Moor. A proposal to extend the canal to join the Bude Agricultural canal was rejected.

The prime objective of Rolle's canal was to carry coal and limestone to be processed inland. Instead of locks to lift or lower them from one level to the next, tub boats capable of carrying four tons of each were fitted with wheels to guide them on rails set in inclined planes. Trains of six tub boats hauled by a horse, in the charge of a man and a boy, could pass each other with barely a foot to spare on either side. There was little risk of drowning in the canal for it was only about four feet deep.

The stone-laying ceremony by Lord Rolle at Beam aqueduct, which carried an inclined plane over the Torridge, nearly ended in tragedy when a cannon, fired to signal the opening of the canal, exploded seriously wounding the cannoneer. The completed canal cost his Lordship £50,000 and it is unlikely that his investment ever yielded a profit. Within 50 years, competition from the Bideford-Torrington railway had forced its closure.

Within nine years of the opening of the Stockton and Darlington railway in 1822,

prominent citizens of Bideford and Okehampton set up a committee to examine the
feasibility of engineering a narrow gauge railway linking the two communities. Despite
initial enthusiasm, the discussion came to nothing. In 1845, proposals were floated to
construct a railway from Bideford to Tavistock with branch lines to Barnstaple and
Crediton. Again the project collapsed. Ten years later the North Devon Railway
Company opened a broad gauge line from Crediton to Barnstaple and then to Bideford.

Fig. 18. The inaugural run of the Barnstaple-Bideford Railway.

Local craftsmen and 'cottage industries' were unable to compete with the factory-
produced goods the railway brought into the town. One after the other, limekilns fell
into disuse. Mass-produced chinaware decimated much of the town's once prosperous
pottery industry.

Thrown out of work by agricultural depression, unemployed farmworkers and their
families crowded into Bideford's slums to vie with other jobless men seeking non-
existent work. Their only hope of prosperity was emigration.

The platform for Bideford's involvement in the 19th-century great emigration during
which millions left Britain's shores, was laid in the war year of 1809 with the launching
of the 100-ton, single-masted sloop, *Peter and Sarah* at Richard Chapman's Cleave
Houses shipyard. This sturdy ship was destined to carry some of the first Bideford
emigrants to Newfoundland. Because of a critical shortage of Baltic timber caused by

the French blockade, Chapman had only managed to build one ship during that year. For two years the *Peter and Sarah* traded in the Bristol Channel for her owner, Thomas Husband. In 1811, he sold the ship to Thomas Burnard, a Bideford merchant and thrice mayor of the town. Burnard, with his business interests in Newfoundland, had ambitious plans for his new purchase. He had the *Peter and Sarah* re-rigged as a two-masted brigantine-polucca to enable her to sail to his base at Newfoundland carrying ship-wrights and essential equipment. There he would establish a shipbuilding industry utilising the timber from the colony's vast forests, thereby helping to bypass a critical European timber shortage in the aftermath of the French war.

During August 1818, the *Peter and Sarah* dropped anchor at Richmond Bay, Prince Edward Island. Two years later, William Ellis's first ship arrived back in the Torridge. She was the first of a steady stream of Newfoundland-built ships, some of which were destined to play an important part in the burgeoning emigration trade. Ellis and his apprentices chose to remain at Prince Edward Island, making them among the first Bidefordians to emigrate in the 19th-century's great migration.

The *Peter and Sarah* did not return to Newfoundland but resumed trading in the Bristol Channel. On Burnard's death, the ship passed into the ownership of James Yeo 'the Kilkhampton Carrier', a shipping magnate of humble origins who had made his fortune in Newfoundland. He lived in a fine mansion, Richmond House, which he had built for himself in Appledore, overlooking Richmond dry dock which he had built to fit out his ships. After 50 years' service, the *Peter and Sarah* foundered when she struck rocks at the entrance to Ilfracombe harbour.

Another influential Torridgeside shipowner, Thomas Chanter, a contemporary of James Yeo, operated a fleet of emigrant ships out of Bideford. His Newfoundland-built brigs, *Collina*, *Sapho* and *Euphemia*, were advertised as being: 'conveniently fitted out for families and will take out passengers on moderate terms to Prince Edward Island, Breton, Nova Scotia or New Brunswick'.

In January 1831, 5,000 wellwishers lined Bideford quay to wave *bon voyage* and farewell to relatives and friends emigrating to the New World. Judged by modern standards, conditions aboard were primitive. And 'primitive' varied wildly from the acceptable to the atrocious. The *North Devon Journal* in 1850 describes typical conditions passengers could expect aboard a well managed ship like the Barnstaple-built *Lady Ebrington* (700 tons) which sailed from the Taw with 129 passengers heading for the newly discovered Australian goldfields:

> The height of the between decks varied from six to seven feet according to the size and build of the vessel. It extends the whole inside breadth of the ship, and the berths are fitted along the sides. Each berth contains from six to eight beds one placed above another, that is two people sleeping lengthways with the ship and one, two or four across, according to the capacity of the ship. Along the length of the ship, a table is placed about two and a half feet broad, and securely fastened to the deck in case of heavy weather. Along the sides of passenger ships there are spaces cut out at about every seven feet, and fitted with strong glass panes, which can be pushed outwards for the purpose of ventilation. These panes of glass are about six inches in diameter and the berths are frequently so fitted that one pane serves as light for two cabins. Of course these small windows are chiefly useful in heavy rains when it is impossible to open the hatches.

The wife of a skilled shipwright of Ilfracombe described the experiences of her passage to Australia in a letter to her father:

> We left Plymouth on the 7th February, 1849, and arrived in Melbourne on the 6th June after a long and tedious voyage. My dear father, I think I was the best sailor of the lot; Philip was sick a day or

two; John and Isaac were quite at home; Mary, Eliza, and Ellen were very well; but on board is a miserable place for children. We had a very good captain, and a very bad doctor. We had six births, and seven deaths; one woman from Bideford, by the name of Croker, died with an inflammation, the rest were children. We had plenty of food, but the little girl's teeth were not strong enough to eat the biscuits. The water got very bad. We found it very hot when crossing the line; the weather came into a calm and we lay on one place for three weeks; I thought all must have died with the heat. Philip and the boys slept on deck. The sailors caught a quantity of fish and four sharks and ate them. I saw one whale myself, but the sailors frequently saw them; and a quantity of birds of all kinds. We caught seabirds that would measure from ten to twelve feet from wing to wing, they were very good for eating. We had one gale; we could not carry any canvas for three days; then we got into a cold climate.

At the nether end of the scale, the maggot-ridden *Ticonderoga*, 700 tons, carrying 811 impoverished Scots who had been ousted from their crofts in the Highland clearances of the 1850s[2] to Australia, was condemned as being a plague ship. Ninety-six of her passengers died of cholera, smallpox and dysentery on the voyage. Although of equal tonnage to the *Lady Ebrington*, it will be noted that the *Ticonderoga* carried 682 more passengers.

Not infrequently excessive drinking among the crew caused horrific disasters in otherwise seaworthy emigrant ships. On the night of 3 May 1855, the *John*, Captain Rawle, bound from Plymouth to America with 263 emigrants, some from the Bideford area, smashed headlong on the Manacle reef off St Keverne on the Lizard. The drunken crew fought off passengers for places in the lifeboats. While all the crew were saved, only 70 passengers survived. Rawle, whom witnesses accused of being drunk at the time of the wrecking, was found guilty of manslaughter and sent to prison. With the exception of a steward who had shown conspicuous gallantry, the crew were reprimanded for cowardice and inhuman behaviour.

What of the fortunes of those who reached Australia to start a new life? A namesake of the woman Croker, who had died during the voyage of the *Lady Ebrington*, had set off into the Australian hinterland with his last threepenny piece in his pocket. Within a year of reaching the Ballarat goldfields he had managed to save £4,000. John Bray and Thomas Harris from Weare Giffard discovered a gold nugget weighing 85lbs. No wonder the two men rang the bells of Weare Giffard church on their return to the village. Anne Barrow of Bideford sold her wedding bonnet to help pay the £5 fare for a ride on a bullock cart to the goldfields while her husband, John, did the journey on foot.

Back home in Bideford a series of cholera epidemics compelled the council to engineer a sewage system which piped the town's residuum into the River Torridge. The prophylactic measures taken to prevent the spread of cholera from infected areas were primitive and virtually useless. To disinfect the air barrels of tar were burnt in infected zones. Lime was spread in the alleys and streets; buildings were limewashed, and drinking wells capped. People complained that the combined smell of burning tar and the smoke from the bonfires of infected clothing and bedding was worse than the stench of death itself.

A sick dispensary for the poor had opened in Buttgarden Street. The Town Hall had been rebuilt in an Elizabethan style. It incorporated a public reading room and, in the basement, cells for prisoners. In an age of growing religious tolerance, nonconformist chapels[3] had sprung up all over the town. The first issue of Thomas Honey's local newspaper, the *Bideford Gazette*, appeared on 1 January 1856. A literary and scientific institute, a debating society and a gardening society flourished. A music hall capable of accommodating 600 had been inaugurated in Bridgeland Street. For the brutally minded, free entertainment was provided at the army garrison camped in Drum Field, Old Town, when defaulting soldiers were publicly flogged with the cat o' nine tails. The Bideford Anthracite Mining and Mineral Black Paint operated a mine at East-the-Water. The ore was transferred direct into colliers by a shute crossing the Barnstaple road adjacent to Restarick's shipyard. Lumps of ore falling from the shute became a public danger. The town council warned the company that proceedings would be taken against it if it did not rectify the situation. Another heavy industry, Henry Tardrew's Ironfoundry, manufacturers of ironmongery and grates, carried on business at 9 High Street.

In 1801, the town's population amounted to 2,987; 70 years later it had more than doubled to 6,969 people. The population was divided into 3,224 males and 3,745 females. One thousand, six hundred and seventy-five families lived in 1,355 houses on 3,196 acres. Sixty-eight paupers were housed in the workhouse. Besides these inmates, the workhouse held 16 blind persons of whom four had been blind from birth. There were 15 deaf mutes, 29 imbeciles and six lunatics.

A.J. Munby, a Victorian barrister with a roving eye, visited Bideford in the 1860s. He described the Longbridge as the finest medieval bridge he had ever seen. He wrote of *Chester's Hotel* (Tantons) and Eliza Tyzack as being 'a reasonable inn with a female waiter [Eliza] tall, buxom, six and twenty but looked less'. He visited Chudleigh's derelict Civil War fort at East-the-Water. He took:

> a narrow footpath which led me through a farm . . . Just above the fort, a small square enclosure jutting from the hill, and surrounded by low battlements. From it an excellent view of the bridge and the river below, and Bideford on the opposite slope. The tide was low, and the stream had become a mere runlet among the wastes of firm sand on which lay the boats and a few vessels.

He found the market consisted of:

> . . . rows of tiled shed and paths between; and it was market day. There was not much costume, but there was affectation. The farmers' daughters mostly wore white or yellow jackets and round mushroom hats; but their hands were bare and ruddy and their figures stout, and they carried big baskets, and rode a-horseback not unfrequently, and their daughters made excellent saleswomen behind their stalls spread with poultry, eggs, and vegetables. The servant girls dressed as such, in coarse rustic straw bonnets, and gay shawls. There were many pleasant faces and broad shoulders but not much beauty. The whole building buzzed with a hustling, good natured crowd of women; and outside were the men, looking after the horse and pig market. It was interesting and on the whole very satisfactory.

His perambulations took him to Northam which he described as:

> Once a town, still large and well built, picturesque old houses, rustic streets. The church, finely decorated, and well restored; Elizabethan school close by. On an open space overlooking the vale, I fell in love with a sturdy little wench, going with a pail of water and singing as she went. Age 13, but looked about a woman; bonnet a-tilt, short rough hair all blown about her face; name Mary Mudd.

He wrote of Barnstaple as being commonplace; Instow as a new white village; praised Fairy Cross as a pretty hamlet in a hollow, but dismissed Horns Cross as a common village. At Bucks Mill, he rested and drank from the village stream. At Clovelly, already a tourist attraction, he supped in the kitchen of the *New Inn* where a 'ruddy, stout, little serving wench' brought him beer.

Mary Mudd, A.J. Munby's 'sturdy little wench of Northam' would have known in her later years of the young seaman, Ned Brooks, originally of Brightlingsea, Essex, who had settled in the village, and of the terrible ordeal that befell him in 1884. On 19 May of that year, Ned joined the crew of the 33-ton yacht, *Mignonette*, bound from Southampton to Sydney, Australia. Captained by Thomas Dudley, the crew consisted of Edwin Stephens, mate, Ned Brooks and cabin boy, 17-year-old Richard Parker, from Itchen Ferry, Hampshire.

Fig. 19. Captain Thomas Dudley, Master of the *Mignonette*.

After an uneventful voyage to Funchal, Madeira, where the *Mignonette* was revictualled, the captain set course for the Cape of Good Hope. A few days later, the yacht ran into foul weather. Eventually she was overwhelmed by huge waves but not before the crew had managed to escape in the 14-foot lifeboat. Only by continuous baling could the survivors keep the little craft afloat. Suffering agonies from exposure, the men had to endure the torments of hunger and thirst. Young Richard Parker was delirious and near to death when Dudley, assisted by Stephens, slit the boy's throat with a penknife. Parker's blood was collected in a chronometer case, and although Brooks had taken no part in the murder, he drank his share of the blood. He also joined in eating the boy's flesh which the trio hoped would sustain them until they were rescued. By the time they were picked up by a German barque four days later, they had drifted 1,000 miles. Only a rib bone and fragments of flesh, rotting in the bilges, remained as gruesome evidence of Richard Parker's fate.

On their arrival at Falmouth, Dudley and Stephens were charged with Parker's murder while Ned Brooks chose to give evidence for the Crown. When the melancholy facts behind the killing became public knowledge, a ground swell of sympathy generated for the two men, many people regarding Dudley as a hero who had saved his mates from certain death.

On 6 November 1884 at the Devon and Cornwall Assizes at Exeter, both men were found guilty of murder and Lord Chief Justice Coleridge sentenced them to death. He warned all sailors that they had no defence in law for eating anyone no matter how horrendous the circumstances in which they might find themselves. Their death sentences were commuted to life imprisonment, but after serving only six months in Holloway jail both men were released. Dudley emigrated to Australia where he died from bubonic plague in 1900. Stephens died in 1914. Ned Brooks appeared in ghoulish re-enactments of the tragedy staged in fairground booths. The remains of Richard Parker were interred in the churchyard at Itchen Ferry, where the inscription records his 'dreadful suffering in an open boat in the tropics'.

The Reverend Charles Kingsley's novel *Westward Ho!* with its backdrop of Elizabethan Bideford had been a best-seller for years before young Parker's tragic death.

> All who have travelled through the delicious scenery of North Devon, must needs know the little white town of Bideford, which slopes upwards from its broad tide-river paved with gold sands and many-arched old bridge where the salmon wait for autumn floods . . .

So Kingsley began his famous story, and Bideford is still affectionately known as the 'Little White Town'.

Charles Kingsley was born on 12 June 1819 in the Dartmoor village of Holne where his father was curate. Shortly after his birth, the Kingsleys moved from the village to another curacy. In 1831, the squire of Clovelly, Sir James Hamlyn-Williams, an old friend of the family, offered the vacant living of the village to Charles senior, an offer he gratefully accepted.

The stark contrast between the natural beauty of the North Devon coast and the poverty of the fisherfolk and labourers left an indelible mark on young Charles's political philosophy. While at boarding school in Bristol, he witnessed the bread riots of 1831/2 which reinforced his growing socialist leanings. Finishing his schooling, he read classics and mathematics at King's College, Cambridge. After coming down, he decided to follow his father's footsteps into the Church and returning to Devon, he went into retreat to study theology. After his ordination, he married Fanny Grenfell. In leisure hours he took to writing and his first work was published in 1848. But parochial work combined with his writing undermined his health. When he found a locum to take over his parish of Eversley in Berkshire, he took a long vacation in Bideford to gather background material for a novel he had begun to write. He took a lease on Northdown House, now the Stella Maris Convent, and there, in a first-floor room overlooking the Torridge, he settled down to complete his novel.[4] Seven months and a quarter of a million words later, it was finished. He took the title from a couplet in the first chapter of the book:

Viola   Westward ho! With a rumbelow
          And hurra for the Spanish Main, O!

Fig. 20. Northdown House, where Charles Kingsley wrote *Westward Ho!* It is now the Stella Maris Convent.

Kingsley's love of Bideford and the surrounding countryside extended beyond literature. A close friend of the Bideford doctor, W.H. Ackland, he shared the doctor's concern about the danger which the town's insanitary conditions could cause to health.

When enteric pandemics swept the town in the mid-1850s, Kingsley helped his friend to minister to the sick and dying. He also found time to carry out occasional pastoral duties in Abbotsham and Northam. An accomplished artist, he helped another friend, Edward Capern, Bideford's poet-postman, by giving instruction at art classes at Capern's Mill Street home.

After the publication of *Westward Ho!*, Kingsley returned to Everseley. Novels and religious treatises continued to flow from his pen. By the time of his early death aged 56, Kingsley had become a national figure. Although he espoused socialist principles, he numbered those from all backgrounds, including royalty, among his admirers. On hearing of his death, Queen Victoria wrote in her diary:

OSBORNE, Isle of Wight, 23 Jan. 1875
Poor Canon Kingsley who had been alarmingly ill for the last three or four weeks, died today and is a sad loss. His wife was very ill at the same time, and neither could go to the other, which was dreadfully sad, and terrible for his two daughters. He was full of genius, and energy, noble and warm-hearted, devoted, loyal, and chivalrous, much attached to me and mine, full of enthusiasm, and most kind and good to the poor.

Unveiled in 1906, Charles Kingsley's statue stands at the northern end of Bideford quay within sight of Northdown House. He looks towards the Longbridge which he loved so dearly and holds a manuscript of *Westward Ho!* in his left hand. The little finger of his right hand is missing, broken off by a vandal shortly after the unveiling ceremony.

In breaks from writing *Westward Ho!* Charles Kingsley enjoyed accompanying Edward Capern on his 13-mile round from Bideford post office to Buckland Brewer and back. Capern delivered the mail seven days a week come hail come shine, summer in and winter out. Born in Tiverton in 1819, Edward was taught by his baker father to read and write by the age of nine, a rare accomplishment in an age of mass illiteracy among working people. As a lad, Edward started work in a local factory and later became a shoemaker's apprentice, before turning his skills to carpentry. Despite a vision defect which became progressively worse with age, he developed his artistic talent, and supplemented his income, by portrait painting.

His ambition was to get a steady job where he would be left to his own devices so that he could concentrate on his first love, poetry. At 17, he applied for and was selected for work as a Bideford rural postman. His salary began at 10s.6d. for a seven-day week, later rising to 13s. On this meagre wage, he provided for his devoted wife, 'a charming brunette, intelligent, prudent and good', and their two children, Charles and Milly. Incredibly, the family managed to save a few shillings a week to buy a house. He described his domestic life at their home in Mill Street as being, 'Happy – happy where thousands would be discontented; rich where many would be in want; blessing providence for its bounty, instead of repining for that which has been denied'.

On his rounds delivering the mail, ringing his hand bell to announce his approach, it was his practice to take his lunch break sitting on a roadside bank with a writing pad propped on his satchel jotting down his thoughts, composing verse, or sketching the flora and fauna about him. In his poem, the *Rural Postman*, he wrote of his job:

> O, the postman's is as happy a life
> As any one's I trow;
> Wand'ring away where the dragon-flies play,
> And brooks sing soft and slow;
> And watching the lark as he soars on high,

> To carol in yonder cloud,
> 'He sings in his labour, and why not I?'
> The postman sings aloud.
> And many a brace of humble rhymes
> His pleasant soul hath made,
> Of birds, and flowers, and happy time,
> In sunshine or in shade.

Encouraged by Kingsley, Edward published a collection of his poems. With a foreword written by W.F. Rock, a leading figure in Barnstaple society, Capern's anthology became an immediate success and the first edition of 1,000 was sold out within three months. Queen Victoria, to whom Capern sent a copy, was suitably impressed. The government granted him an annuity of £40, rising to £60, to help him concentrate on his poetry, and the post office recognised their employee's talent by cutting out his Sunday working without loss of pay.

The Caperns moved to Braunton where Edward continued to write prolifically. Incidents in the Crimean War inspired him to compose patriotic verse in the heroic manner so beloved of the Victorians. Among these works was a flowery poem eulogising Britain's victory at the Battle of the Redan guarding the approach to the Russian stronghold of Sebastopol.

Edward Capern – sometimes called the Robert Burns of Devon – died on 24 February 1894. He is buried beside his wife in the cemetery of St Augustine's church, Heanton Punchardon. His postman's bell, now weatherbeaten and in need of preservation, is incorporated in the headstone of his grave.

Among the survivors of the butchery on the glacis leading up the Redan was 24-year-old Captain Henry Hope Crealock of the 90th Light Infantry. Crealock had spent much of his boyhood in Littleham, a parish three miles west of Bideford. When he left Rugby School in 1848, he purchased an army commission. After the Battle of the Redan he was mentioned in despatches for his bravery and was appointed Deputy Adjutant General. Later he was to see action in several minor colonial campaigns as well as taking part in the relief of Europeans besieged in Peking. In 1879, he was given his first active service command – that of Major General commanding the 1st Division of Lord Chelmsford's South African Expeditionary Force fighting Zulu King Cetshwayo's warriors. Already the Zulus had washed their spears in the blood of 800 English dead at Isandhlwana, and had come within a whisker of slaughtering the entire garrison at Rourke's Drift. But by April, the killing power of the Martini-Henry rifle and field artillery had gained ascendency over the Zulus' assegais and knobkerries.

Chelmsford turned from defence to attack. With his army strengthened by 10,000 reinforcements from England, he struck north to destroy Cetshwayo's capital of Ulundi. To conceal his intentions, he ordered Crealock to launch a diversionary advance on the eastern flank. Although the 1st Division was up to strength, its supply train was inadequate. So slow did its advance become, the 1st was derisively dubbed the 'Crealock Crawlers'. During their snail-like progress to the Indian Ocean, Crealock's men did not encounter any hostile Zulus or suffer any battle casualties. However, 497 officers and men had to be evacuated to base hospitals suffering from fevers, while 71 other victims were buried along the route.

After destroying Ulundi, Wolseley met up with Crealock. He made it abundantly clear to his subordinate that for all the good it had accomplished in the campaign, the 1st Division might have remained in England. For this military fiasco, Crealock was created a Companion of the Order of St Michael and St George and awarded a campaign medal with clasp. After 40 years' service, Crealock retired from the army with the rank of Lieutenant General.

While on active service in South Africa, he had supplied the *Illustrated London News* with sketches of the war. At the time of his death, he was engaged in writing and illustrating *Deer Stalking in the Highlands of Scotland*, the definitive Victorian work on sport.

His body was taken back to Littleham for interment in the 15th-century church of St Swithun where his alabaster effigy lies on an elaborate tomb sculpted by Mr. Temple Moore of London. The village inn, the *Crealock Arms*, serves as a reminder of the exploits of a largely forgotten general from a half-remembered colonial war.

At the time when Henry Crealock clambered up the bloodstained slope to the Russian Redan, Captain John Hanning Speke (1827-64) of Orleigh Court, Buckland Brewer served with a Turkish regiment at Kerch on the eastern flank of the Crimean peninsula.

A descendant of Charles Speke who had been hanged in Ilminster, Somerset, for his involvement in the Monmouth rebellion, John was baptised at the parish church of St Mary and St Benedict, Buckland Brewer. He received his early education at Barnstaple Grammar School. Later, he boarded at Blackheath College, South London where his education was tailored for an army career. Joining the Indian army at 17, he saw active service in several minor wars. Promoted to lieutenant in 1850, he was appointed captain two years later. In 1854, he volunteered for the Crimea. At the end of hostilities, he joined Lieutenant Richard Burton, with whom he had made a previous trip to the Horn of Africa, to discover the source of the Nile at the fabled Fountain of Coy. After weeks of danger, hardship and disappointment, the pair found themselves at Tabora in modern Tanzania. Here they heard of a great lake hitherto undiscovered by white men which lay three days' march away. Although weak from illness, the two men set out to find the lake. After an uneventful journey, they arrived on the shores of a vast inland sea. Speke concluded that the sea formed the reservoir of the legendary Fountain of Coy; in spite of Burton's scepticism, he named the lake 'Victoria' to honour his monarch.

During the following year, Speke, now a national hero, returned to the lake with James Augustus Grant. This time he found a waterfall near modern Kampala which he named the Ripon Falls in honour of the President of the Royal Geographical Society. Here indeed was the true birthplace of the great Nile.

In September 1864 Speke died from accidental gunshot wounds sustained while hunting partridges, and he is buried at Dawlish Wake, near Chard, Somerset. His claim to have discovered the Fountain of Coy was confirmed by later explorers, notably by Henry Stanley and David Livingstone's expedition to Lake Victoria.

Numbered among the greatest heroes of the Crimean War was 20-year-old Gunner/Driver Thomas Arthur of Greencliff Cottage, Abbotsham. Ironically he escaped the death sentence by the skin of his teeth for committing a deed of bravery which was to be recognised by the award of the Victoria Cross, the country's premier decoration for bravery.

Thomas Arthur enlisted in the Royal Regiment of Artillery during the 1850s. In 1855 he found himself on active service in the Crimea outside Sebastopol. On 7 June, he was ordered to guard the battery's supply dump while his mates engaged the enemy. Towards evening, he noticed that nearby embattled infantrymen were running low on ammunition. Disregarding his orders, and indifferent to his own safety, he carried forward ball and ammunition over bullet-swept ground. For abandoning his post, Arthur was threatened with an immediate court martial and a dawn appointment with the hangman. Luckily for him, his bravery had been noticed by the Colonel of Infantry who interceded on his behalf. On its institution Arthur was awarded the Victoria Cross. The citation published in the *London Gazette*, 24 February 1857 reads:

> Thomas Arthur, Gunner and Driver, Royal Artillery. When in charge of the magazine in one of the left advanced batteries of the right attack on the 7th June, when the Quarries were taken, he, of his own accord, carried barrels of infantry ammunition for the 7th Fusiliers several times during the evening across the open.
>
> He volunteered for and commanded a party of gunners who spiked Russian cannon at the Redan on 18th June, 1855. Devoted heroism in sallying out of the trenches on numerous occasions and bringing in wounded officers and men.

A year after the end of the war, Gunner Arthur, together with 61 officers and men, recipients of the V.C., paraded in Hyde Park for a mass investiture ceremony performed by the Queen. Bending down from the saddle of her horse, the Queen pinned the claret red ribbon on the chest of his uniform jacket.

ARTHUR (real name MACARTHUR)
Thomas
Rank: Gunner and Driver
Unit/Force: Royal Regiment of Artillery
Other Decorations: —
Place/Date of Deed: Crimea — 7 and 18 June 1855
Place/Date of Birth: Abbotsham, Bideford, Devon — 1835
Place/Date of Death: Savernake, Wiltshire — 2 Mar. 1902
Place of Memorial: —
Town/County Connections: Bideford, Devon; Savernake, Wiltshire
Remarks: —

BAPTISMS solemnized in the Parish of ___Abbotsham___
in the County of ___Devon___ in the Year 18_36_

When Baptized.	Child's Christian Name.	Parents Name.		Abode.	Quality, Trade, or Profession.	By whom the Ceremony was performed..
		Christian.	Surname.			
August 28 / No. 310.	Thomas	Thomas & Jane	Arthurs	Abbotsham	Labourer	W.R. Heath Walter Curate

Fig. 21.   Baptismal entry and part of service record for gunner/driver Thomas Arthur, V.C.

Arthur fought in the China War of 1860. After serving out his time, he went to live in Savernake, Wiltshire, where he died on 2 March 1902. Shortly after his death, his V.C. was sold for £47.

The sad story of another Bideford character, Captain Henry Clark, who died on 28 April 1836, aged 61, is inscribed on his gravestone, now affixed to the wall of St Mary's church:

> Our worthy friend who lies beneath this stone,
> Was master of a vessel of his own,
> Houses and lands had he, and gold in store,
> He spent the whole and ten times more.
> For twenty years he scarcely slept in bed,
> Linhays and limekilns lulled his weary head,
> Because he would not to the poorhouse go,
> For his proud spirit would not let him go.
> The blackbirds whisterling notes at break of day,
> Used to wake him from his bed of hay,
> Onto the Bridge and Quay he then repaired
> To see what shipping up the river steered.
> Oft in the weeks he used to view the Bridge,
> To see what ships were coming in from the sea,[5]
> To Cap't's wives he brought welcome news,
> And to the relatives of all their crews.
> At last Henry Clark was taken ill,
> And carried off to the workhouse against hil will
> But being of this mortal life quite tired,
> He lived about a month, and then expired.

Another epitaph to a Bideford flirt speaks for itself:

> Here lies the body of Mary Sexton
> Who pleased many a man, but ne'er vex't one,
> Not like the woman who lies under the next stone.

Seven years after Captain Henry's death, a Torridgeside man dedicated an epitaph to a Liverpool schooner, the *John and Lilley*, wrecked off Bideford Bar in a great storm which reached its climax between 14 and 16 January 1843:

> The John and Lilley came ashore
> To feed the hungry and clothe the poor.

Outward bound to West Africa, the *John and Lilley* carried a cargo which included foodstuffs, muskets, cotton ware and other luxuries. For nearly a fortnight the crew fought a losing battle against dirty weather. Blown off course into the Bristol Channel, the schooner lost her rudder and went aground off Bideford Bar where most of the crew managed to struggle ashore. The wrecking tradition of Appledorians had not mellowed over the years. Even before the gale abated, looters swarmed aboard the wreck. A witness to the scene wrote:

The shore was thronged with wreckers, hardened as the rock which surrounded them, wholly intent on plunder. Farmers from this and the adjoining parishes continued through the day to cart off whatever they could put their hands on . . . and I cannot conceive a more useful lesson than condign punishment of some of the more wealthy offenders, some of whom have been more prominent and certainly more wholesale in their proceedings than the numerous poor wretches who might plead their 14 pence a day the amount of a husbandman's wages in this parish.

Fig. 22.   Bideford in the 1860s. Abbotsham Court is given its Old English name, Shebbear-
town—(1). This should not be confused with Shebbear, 15 miles south of Bideford, which
gives its name to Shebbear Hundred. Greencliff Cottage—(2)— was the birthplace of gunner
Thomas Arthur, V.C.

Chapter Six

MODERN TIMES

IN THE EARLY 1860s, the wretchedly poor of Appledore were about to get affluent neighbours, for property developers were poised to cash in on a tourist boom of wealthy Victorians anxious to explore Charles Kingsley's 'Little White Town' of Bideford, and the villages of Northam and Appledore featured in *Westward Ho!*.

On 25 March 1863, the Northam Burrows (North Devon) Hotel and Villa Building Co. Ltd., was floated to exploit 75 acres of farmland overlooking the Pebble Ridge as a 'fashionable watering place'. At the suggestion of Charles Kingsley's old friend, Dr. Ackland, the development was to be known as 'Westward Ho!'. The company intended to build a prestige resort to rival the luxury of Ilfracombe and Torquay. In February 1864, the mayor of Bideford watched the company chairman's wife lay the foundation stone of the *Westward Ho! Hotel*, the centrepiece of the development.

Kingsley was concerned that the scheme would be detrimental to the environment. He wrote to Ackland: 'How goes Northam Burrows scheme for spoiling that beautiful place with hotels and villas? You will frighten away all the seapies,[1] and defile the Pebble Ridge with chicken bones and sandwich scraps . . .'. The great novelist need not have worried. Not for these developers the bucket and spade or junk-food image of 20th-century Westward Ho!

While the hotel was under construction, the Northam Burrows Promenade and Landing Pier Company, chaired by J. Pine Coffin, was floated, its objective being to raise capital to build a 600-foot pier at the western end of the resort. Cash poured in and the engineering began, and even before the structure was finished the pleasure steamer *Spicy*, packed with half-day trippers from Bideford, sailed to view it.

However, misfortune dogged the venture. October gales destroyed all but 150 feet of its length and an attempt to rebuild a shortened pier ended in disaster when a storm pounded it to pieces. But the company stuck to its task and the pier was finally opened to the public on 24 July 1873. Seven years later winter storms completely and irrevocably destroyed it.

Beneath Northam Cliffs, the United Services College (U.S.C.) for the sons of gentlefolk opened in 1874, together with an associated junior school at nearby Buckleigh. Rudyard Kipling, the distinguished author and ex-U.S.C. pupil, based his best-selling novel *Stalky and Co.* on his schooldays at the College. A property tycoon, George Molesworth, saw the profitability of providing a covered swimming pool for the use of both the Collegians and the public when a dip in the bay was ruled out by the weather or time of year. His Grand Nassau Bath measured 133 by 33 feet.[2] A roller skating track surrounded the pool.

The Westward Ho! Company donated the site and assisted in the finance for building Holy Trinity church, consecrated by the Bishop of Exeter on 24 March 1870. Gentlemen's residences sprang up behind the broad sweep of the Pebble Ridge. Many of them were owned by former regular army officers who had seen active service in the Crimea. Retired senior N.C.O.s dominated the top managerial positions in the resort. Ex-Sergeant Lewis drilled barrack square discipline into the red-jacketed boy caddies at the North Devon and West of England Golf Club founded in 1863, which made it only the second course that existed south of the Scottish border. Ex-Sergeant Major Keyte presided as the postmaster in Nelson Terrace while Ex-Sergeant Murray managed Mr. Molesworth's genteel *Rowenna* Guest House. At the bottom of the pecking order came the menials such as ostlers, grooms and stable lads who lived in accommodation well removed from the villas of their masters, and where an ale house had been opened for their refreshment.

International celebrities who visited the resort in the early days included the Shah of Persia; the German Chancellor, Count Otto von Bismarck; the exiled Dauphin of France; and the Prince of Egypt. Because of patronage by the Prince of Wales, the golf club was granted the right to prefix 'royal' to its title.

Barely two miles from the swanky luxury of Westward Ho! were the poverty-stricken villages of Appledore and Irsha where:

> the inhabitants are as wild and uncivilised a set as any to be found in this part of the Kingdom and where, till lately, a stranger could not pass without insult. Shoes and stockings are here unknown luxuries to the younger portion of the population and the women may be seen sitting outside their doors in the streets working (or more frequently quarrelling) as is seen in the South of Europe.

Premier Disraeli's concept of an England divided into two nations – rich and poor – is clearly exemplified here.

Underprivileged children of North Devon not only went to school shoeless, but often without food to tide them through the day. To alleviate their hunger, they sucked round pebbles called 'saviours'.

Neither deprived Appledore nor wealthy Westward Ho! had a railway link with the London and South Western Railway's main line station at Bideford, and in 1898 the Bideford, Appledore and Westward Ho! Railway Company (B.A.W.Ho!R.) was floated to rectify this situation. The company accepted a £50,000 tender to engineer a standard gauge railway. The council had demanded that a narrow gauge line, to run from Bideford to Northam and eventually to end at Appledore, should be built. On 21 April 1901, the *North Devon Journal* reported on the inaugural non-stop run when the 27-ton locomotive, *Grenville*, hauled two carriages from Bideford to Northam. Appledore was not to be connected to the line until 1908. The *North Devon Journal* reported:

> A start was made from the North West end of Short Bank at Curtis's Marsh, and thence the line curls round to Chanter's Road and Northam Causeway. At each place, after the line is opened, a stop will be made to take up passengers . . . The train was soon passing along under Raleigh Hill with North Down Hill a short distance on and Kenwith, the residence of Mrs. Pine Coffin, and Cornborough, the residence of Maj. Gen. Boyce, are seen on the right, while a little further on is Abbotsham Court, the residence of one of the promoters of the line, George Taylor. Immediately after, a splendid view of the bay is opened up. As the train rounds the Cornborough cliffs, the northern side of the bay is seen. The train runs along at parts but a few feet from the very edge of

the cliff, the track having been excavated from the solid rocks. There is a station just below the *Grand Hotel* and the United Services College and the terminus is situated just below the Golf Pavilion and under the village of Northam.

Yesterday a speed of 36 m.p.h. was obtained between Bideford and Westward Ho!, the journey being done in about 10 minutes. The Bideford Season Band (Herr Croop's German band) played selections *en route* and at Westward Ho! In the Westward Ho! station teas were provided by the Company, Mr. Galliford supplying the victuals.

The carriages were built in Bristol . . . on the central corridor system. They are comfortably upholstered in American leather (1st Class) and cloth (3rd Class). Each carriage will seat 10 first and 40 third class passengers. There is no second class. They are nicely decorated with teak outside panels and polished oak inside. The engines (*Kingsley*, *Torridge* and *Grenville*) were built by the Hunslet Engine Co. of Leeds, and are sufficiently powerful to draw 100 tons. The fares will be, through to Northam, 1st Class: single 8d., return 1s.0d.; 3rd Class: single 5d., no 3rd Class return.

Unable to cross the Torridge to make a connection with the L.S.W.R. station at East-the-Water, the company had to be content with a terminus on the quay close to the bottom of Cooper Street. A booking office and waiting room operated from premises now occupied by Peter Adams, Estate Agents. Because the railway track ran along the public highway, the locomotives were fitted with 'cow-catchers' and wheelguards to prevent injury to the public.

Difficulties had beset the company since its inception. The contractor had been sacked when expenditure soared to £57,000, leaving the company on the verge of bankruptcy. The British Electric Traction took it over, allowing it to retain its corporate identity. The company's relationship with the town council, who had originally expressed enthusiasm for the line, had deteriorated and now councillors and other influential citizens feared that the town's environment and their properties would be devalued by trains rattling along the quay puffing out clouds of dirty smoke.

The bitterest dispute the company had with the town council arose out of a collision between an engine and a pony-and-trap. The council refused them permission to lay a loop line on the quay to lessen danger to the public by making it easier to manoeuvre their rolling stock. Early on a Sunday morning the company took the law into their own hands. While Bidefordians enjoyed a weekend lie-in, railway navvies ripped up a length of the quay and began to lay the loop. Aroused by the noise, irate townspeople converged on the quay to confront the railwaymen. Tempers flared and scuffles broke out. To prevent a breach of the peace, extra police were drafted into the town. The town clerk took the first train to London to apply successfully for a High Court injunction against the company. The court ordered the B.W.Ho! & A.R. to immediately remove the rails and reinstate the quay. When Board of Trade Inspectors examined the line in 1904, they over-ruled Bideford council by sanctioning the loop to be made as a safety precaution.

With passenger fares undercut by road transport, an unimaginative timetable, and a failure to attract freight trade, the B.W.Ho! & A.R. rarely showed a profit. To try and boost passenger trade the company erected a music hall on Westward Ho! station platform. During the summer of 1908, the 'Jolly Dutch Entertainers and Clog Dancers' entertained the public. A proposal to extend the line to Bucks Cross, Clovelly and Hartland so as to cash in on the booming tourist trade came to nothing. The final blow to the company's viability came with the soaring cost of coal on the outbreak of the Kaiser's War.

In March 1917, the government requisitioned the three engines and rails of the B.W.Ho! & A.R. for war service in Flanders. On Sunday 29 July, Bidefordians turned

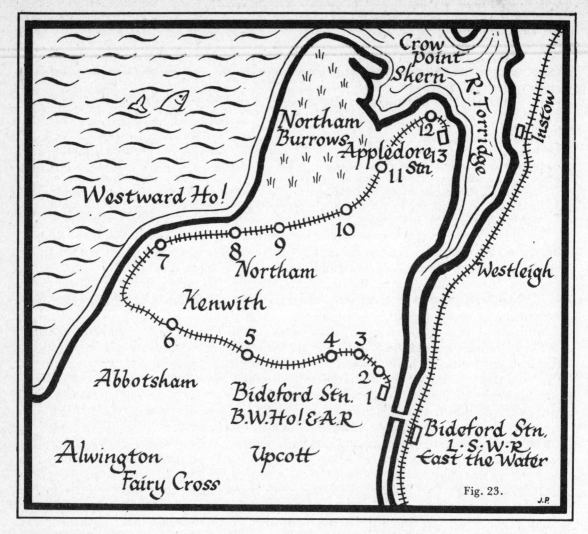

Fig. 23.

J.P.

ROUTES of L·S·W·R & B·WHo! & RAILWAYS

1 Bideford-Quay Terminus
2 Strand Halt
3 Yard Halt (Kingsley Rd)
4 Causeway Crossing
5 Kenwith Castle Halt
6 Abbotsham Rd. Station
7 Cornborough Cliffs Halt

8 Westward Ho! Station
9 Beach Road Halt
10 Northam Station
11 Richmond Rd. Halt
12 Lovers Lane Halt
13 Appledore Station

out to bid farewell to the *Torridge*, the *Kingsley* and the *Grenville* as the locomotives rumbled over the Longbridge on temporary railway lines. A number of rail gangers, overcome by emotion, were later fined for drinking after licensing hours. The locomotives went to the army supply depot at Avonmouth. It is known that the *Grenville* and the *Torridge* were loaded aboard an army supply ship with the unlikely name of *S.S. Gotterdamerung* for shipment to France. Off Padstow, the *Gotterdamerung* was sunk by a U-boat.

Kingsley survived the war, and was sold by the Ministry of Munitions to the National Smelting Company. She was scrapped in 1937. The carriages were sold by auction in 1921. Sliced in half, one of the carriages ended its life as two beach huts on Westward Ho! beach near Molesworth's Nassau Bath. Another found its way to Bedfordshire.

Among the visible remains of the old B.W.Ho! & A.R. are the engine and rolling stock sheds in Kingsley Road, now used as a dairy and transport depot. Kingsley Road was built over the route of the railway. The outlines of fireplaces of the waiting rooms of Appledore station are etched in a ruined wall at Torridge Road, while the site of Westward Ho! station is now the bus terminal, Nelson Road.

When the *Torridge* returned from Westward Ho! in July 1905 with a detachment of the North Devon Yeomanry who had been training on the Burrows, her carriages would have been lit by hissing acetylene lamps. Gas lamps lit Bideford's Longbridge and quay.[3] Electric lighting grew in popularity in the town in the Edwardian era before the First World War; however the majority of householders had to suffice with paraffin and candles for lighting. Home-made bread was mostly baked in cloam ovens or 'Bodley' cooking ranges. Water was boiled in iron cauldrons suspended over cooking fires. Field labourers worked a minimum of 10 hours a day, seven days a week, with no overtime payment, for 12s.0d. (60p). At harvest time work began at dawn and finished at dusk for which the labourer might be lucky enough to receive an extra £1. Several herds of cattle were kept within the town's boundaries. Mr. Williams, who grazed his cows off Abbotsham Road, kept his animals in a shippon behind the *Ring of Bells* public house in Honestone Street. He sold milk from the churn to people living in the market area. Thomas Stevens, blacksmith, had his smithy nearby.

The cattle market was held on a Tuesday. At that time the market lay between Meddon Street and Honestone Street. Butchers slaughtered animals on their premises often in unhygienic conditions, and meat had to be sold and consumed quickly before it went putrid. The Pannier Market presented a colourful and bustling spectacle as farmers' wives brought farm produce for sale, bakers sold freshly baked bread, fishmongers and butchers displayed their wares, colporteurs did a brisk trade selling religious missives to the pious and itinerant cheapjacks hawked their shoddy goods.

The market was a popular venue to meet up with friends or to tuck into a plate of pork and pickles washed down with 'dishes' of tea in the eating rooms. Local inns and hotels offered a lunch of roast beef and vegetables for 1s.0d. (5p), or roast duck with trimmings at 1s.6d. (7½p). A Hungarian band paraded the streets playing popular tunes. A hurdy-gurdy man complete with a performing monkey was a childrens' favourite.

Several family businesses trading in the early 1900s flourished in the 1980s. These include Pridham's, saddlers of Grenville Street; Merefield & Trapnells, of the High Street (now Trapnells), haberdashers who drew their clientele from the well-to-do; further down the hill, townspeople favoured the haberdashery of Messrs. Chopes. George Boyles,[4] ladies' and gentlemen's outfitters, at the junction of the High Street

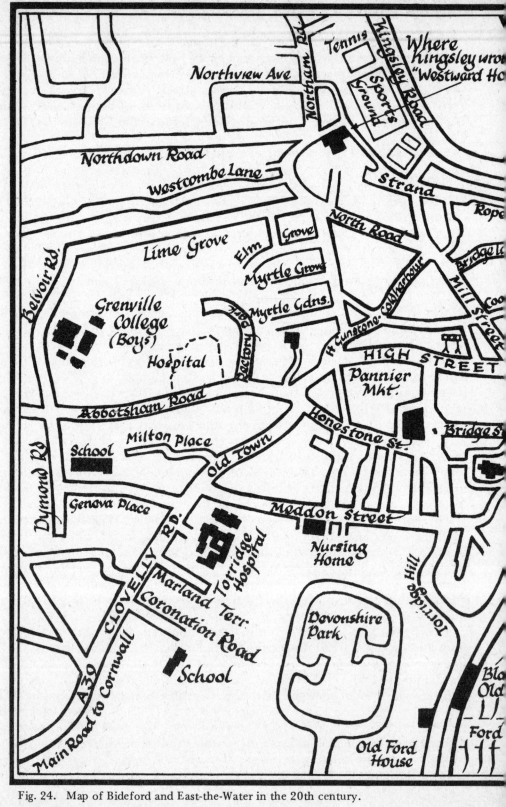

Fig. 24. Map of Bideford and East-the-Water in the 20th century.

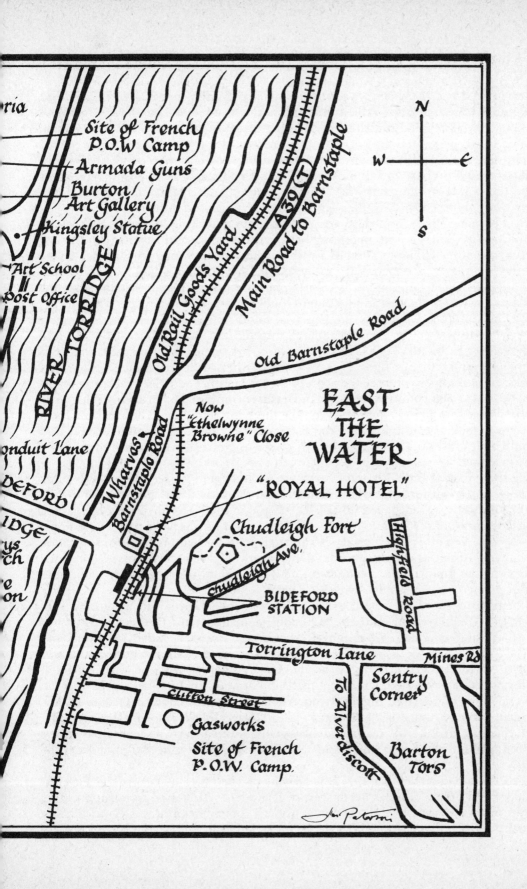

and Allhalland Street, drew custom from farmers and country gentry. Wickham Bros., brewers, supplied intoxicants to the public and to the trade. Descendants of R. & R.G. Giddy, corn merchants and maltsters of Meddon Street, now control Bideford Carpet Services of Bridgeland Street.

At the quay, the *S.S. Devonia* which operated a bi-weekly service between Bideford and Bristol, would prepare to sail on the tide. A council steamroller positioned on the quay had the task of levelling out wheel-ruts in the mud and pebble road surface. Road sweepers were perpetually shovelling up horse droppings and rubbish.

During February 1910, Appledore was plunged into mourning by the tragedy of the sinking of Messrs. Bailey's ferry operating between Appledore and Instow with the loss of a ferryman, father of eight, Thomas Edward Fishwick, and two passengers. At the inquest the sole survivor, Albert Vaggers, recounted how the ferry had been overwhelmed by a squall when only 50 yards from Appledore quay. The jury found that the drowning had been accidental, and no blame could be attached to anyone. The coroner expressed the court's sympathy to the bereaved families.

Eighteen months after the Appledore ferry tragedy, the catastrophe of the 1914-18 war, in which an estimated 10,000 Devonians died, broke out. After an initial surge of young men volunteering to fight in a war which they believed would be over by Christmas, the stream of volunteers dried up. By the summer of 1915, recruiting teams scouring the towns and countryside of North Devon encountered a hardening reluctance among the farmers to permit their sons to take the King's shilling. They wanted them on the farm to look after the animals and crops. The young men themselves said that they would wait until the Germans got a bit closer to North Devon before they would consider enlisting.

Among those men of Bideford and district who volunteered for service was Frederick Johns, born at Huddisford, Woolfardisworthy, on 21 May 1891. Shortly before the outbreak of hostilities, Fred signed up as a Territorial in the 16th North Devon Hussars, based on Torrington. In August 1914, No. 905 Trooper Johns was packed into Barnstaple Drill Hall with 1,400 other Territorials. No arrangements for bedding, food or sanitation had been made. After this chaotic introduction to army life, Fred and his mates entrained for Clacton on the first leg of a great adventure which would take them half-way round the world. Many of them would never see Devon again.

After helping to guard the east coast from a threatened German invasion, the 16th sailed for the Mediterranean and the Gallipoli peninsula. On 21 August 1915, they waded ashore at Suvla Bay. After initial success, the invasion ended in failure and trench warfare. During the winter, Fred suffered frostbite to his toes and feet and was hospitalised in Malta where he made a complete recovery. While he was in Malta, Gallipoli had been evacuated. Fred rejoined his battalion in Egypt; here he met up with several of his mates from Bideford and Woolfadisworthy including George Bailey, Alf Bowden, Henry Frain, Josiah Hayman, John Hearn, Job Prouse and Arthur Allin. Now reformed as an infantry regiment, the Devons formed part of General Allenby's Egyptian Expeditionary Force which had the objective of liberating Palestine from the Turks.

Towards the end of November 1917, the Devons reached the outskirts of the Turkish-held village of El Foka, 50 miles north-west of Jerusalem. Distressed from suppurating sand-sores, Fred was sent to the rear for treatment shortly before the Devons made a night attack on the village. After 12 hours of bitter fighting, the Devons were forced to withdraw to avoid encirclement and further unnecessary casualties. Five officers and 140 men had been killed or were missing, nine officers and 32 men wounded; which totalled nearly 40% of the battalion's establishment. Among the dead were George Bailey, Alf Bowden, Henry Frain, Josiah Hayman and Job Prouse. Arthur Allin was severely wounded in the leg.

After the capture of Jerusalem, Fred, now fully recovered, returned to the Devons who were sent to the Western Front to join in the pursuit of the German armies, retreating after the failure of their March 1918 offensive. Fred took part in the storming of the Hindenburg Line, and the capture of Moislins village where John Hearn was killed.

Now a corporal, Fred ended the war at Grammond, Belgium. With the exception of frostbite and sand-sores, he had survived the whole war without a scratch. Demobilised in 1919, he worked on the roads for the Bideford rural council. He helped in rescue work at the Lynton flood disaster in 1953. Now aged 93 and widowed, he tends his garden at Bucks Cross.

Between 1914 and 1918, 18 steamships and two sailing vessels had sunk in Bideford Bay, 13 of which were attributed to enemy action. The first vessel to be sunk, *S.S. Bayonne*, fell victim to U-boat 65, who followed up her success by sinking *S.S. Queenswood*. The largest ship to be torpedoed was the 7,388-ton *S.S. Rewa*, a hospital ship homeward-bound from Madrid to Avonmouth.

Cook & Son of Richmond Yard, Appledore, fitted out the auxiliary motored schooner, *Sidney*, as a decoy 'Q' ship with concealed armament to ambush U-boats, and she was credited with sinking U.39 off the Isle of Wight. Another ship utilised as a 'Q' ship, the 64-ton *Bridesmaid*, had been launched at Restarrick's East-the-Water yard in 1882. Equipped with a 12lb. gun and renamed *George L. Muir*, she ostensibly traded as a North Sea tramp, but never engaged the enemy.

A crash government programme to replace shipping lost to enemy action began in 1917. The Restarrick Yard won a contract to build four standardised cargo ships of 482 tons each. The first to be launched was the *Orchis* in 1918, followed by the *Ortona*, the *Orleigh* and the *Orenie*. After the Armistice, Cooks purchased the four ships and operated them as a coastal trading fleet.

On the home front, Bideford and Northam boy scouts acted as messenger boys for a Royal Flying Corps detachment based on Northam Burrows. Armed with broomsticks, the boys also mounted guard on the Buckleigh waterworks. Together with the coast-guards, they patrolled lonely stretches of beaches and cliff tops. Many wounded soldiers recuperated from their injuries in Torridgeside hospitals and convalescent homes.

Demobilised Bideford servicemen returning to the town found that it had changed little. The cattle market was still held in the Honestone-Meddon Street area. The shopping centre revolved about the post office then in the High Street. The surface of many streets had yet to be metalled. Horse transport predominated over the internal combustion engine. Sub-standard housing existed in the town centre. There were two cinemas, the *Palladium* in Mill Street with seats available at 2d. and the *Palace* in Bridgeland Street. The *Palladium* closed down in 1922, and the foyer is now Patt's greengrocery and the auditorium is used as storage space. The *Palace* remained in business until the late 1960s when it was first converted into a supermarket and then into a furniture store.

In the mid-1920s, pony racing became a popular attraction for Bidefordians when the National Pony Turf Club opened a seven furlong track close to the Abbotsham Cliffs at Cornborough. During 1924, six meetings were held. The Whit Sunday card listed 45 starters spread over five races. The prize money was modest; the winner took 12 guineas and the third four guineas. Because of its isolation and lack of transport facilities, the course never attracted enough outside patronage to make it profitable. Shunned by the horse-racing governing bodies, the Pony Turf Club was forced to disband, and for a period the track was used for greyhound racing. The restaurant and offices of the defunct track survive as a private residence. However, pony racing did not entirely disappear from the Bideford social calendar, for as a potboiler to the annual Regatta, impromptu racing took place on the sandbanks at East-the-Water, exposed at low tide.

After years of neglect, the fabric of the Longbridge had deteriotated to an alarming degree. The self-indulgence of the Bridge Trustees was also blamed for the bridge's deplorable state. Charles Kingsley had earlier written that the Longbridge was:

> . . . an inspired bridge, a soul saving bridge, an educational bridge, a sentinent bridge, and last, but not least, a dinner giving bridge . . . The bridge has from time to time founded charities, built schools, waged lawsuits, and finally given yearly dinners, and kept for that purpose, (luxurious and liquorous that it was) the best stocked cellar of wine in Devon.

The cost of essential work was estimated at £20,000, a sum the Trust could not afford. The Trustees turned to Bideford town council for financial assistance. Although the economy of the town largely depended on the bridge's safety, the council disclaimed moral responsibility for its upkeep, claiming that Devon county council's Bridges and Main Roads Committee must be held equally liable for its maintenance. Devon county council voted £7,000 to the cost provided that Bideford council agreed to match their contribution with a 'reasonable' sum. After months of haggling, a compromise was thrashed out and work began.

The carriageway was widened from 14 feet 9 inches to 16 feet, with an extra 7 feet for pavements, and the Victorian ironwork was replaced by stone. When the work had been completed, Gurnay's ancient Longbridge was capable of carrying 10-ton vehicles.

Over the years since the Potato Riots, Bidefordians had lost none of their independence and volatility. In the spring of 1913 a near riot occurred at a meeting of the National Union of Women's Suffrage Society (non-militant) at the Town Hall held under the presidency of the Rev. G. Scholey of Appledore. Men and women crowding the public gallery booed the assembly even before the meeting had begun. The Chairman, Miss Walford, did her best to carry on business above the din which reached a crescendo when a speaker singled out Mrs. Hamblyn of Clovelly Court as an example of a gentle lady who should be allowed to vote. The hecklers shouted back that the suffragettes wanted to confine the franchise to upper-class ladies and deny it to working-class women. Nonagenarian Captain Molesworth thrashed the council table with his walking stick demanding order. Against a background of continuous hubbub, the Captain declared that although he had lived in the district for half a century, he had never known Bideford people to behave so disgracefully. Despite the disorder, the Committee managed to pass a resolution in favour of women's suffrage. Replying to a vote of thanks, Miss Walford blamed the disturbance on hooligans from outside the town.

A hostile demonstration met the members when they left the hall and police had to escort their motor cars through the crowd. The franchise was extended in 1918 to women over 30 so that they could vote in the General Election.

Throughout the 1920s, Bideford celebrated an annual reminder of the bad old days of limited parliamentary franchise. The 'Shamwickshire Election'[3] ridiculing local political life took place annually in November when a mock 'mayor' and 'mayoress' (both male) were 'elected'. The ceremony probably had its origins in Barnstaple-born John Gay's (1685-1732) *Beggar's Opera* which related low-life criminality to high-life political corruption. The first 'Shamwickshire' election was held at Garrat Village, Wandsworth, London, after a particularly controversial parliamentary election.

The festivities began in East-the-Water with shipwrights ringing handbells and firing maroons from East-the-Water amid scenes of boisterous buffoonery. After their election, the mayor and his mayoress, seated in a cart, were hauled across the Longbridge for a tour of their demesne. Before them went men and boys rolling blazing tar barrels. The procession made frequent stops for liquid refreshment and increasingly drunken speechmaking.

In the mid-1930s the rowdiness of the 'Shamwickshire' celebrations gave offence to the dignity of the town council, and the ceremony was suppressed. An East-the-Water football team 'Shamwickshire' keeps the memory of the old jollifications in the town. Another custom to disappear was the 'Beat the Clock' race run on the eve of the Bideford Regatta when competitors had to cross the Longbridge during the time that the town clock was striking eight in the evening. The custom has been superseded by the 'Round the Town' race.

An anthracite seam discovered at the base of Cornborough Cliffs in the 19th century excited commercial interest in the 1920s. At a time of serious economic depression, the matter was raised in question time in the House of Commons. The questioner asked the Secretary of Mines:

> If the Minister's attention had been drawn to the discovery of a seam of anthracite coal near Bideford, and whether any steps to develop the seam had come to the knowledge of the Department? Colonel Lane replied he was aware operations had been in progress in the neighbourhood of Bideford with the object of opening out workable seams of anthracite.

The scheme came to nothing. Perhaps the questioner had in mind the development of an alternative industry to absorb Bideford workers who had been made redundant by the depression, including those thrown on the dole by the failure of one of the town's biggest employers, Vincent & Duncan, collarmakers of Westcombe Lane. Together with its Appledore factory, Vincent's had employed over 600 people at the height of its success.

Originally a water-powered cornmill, Vincent's building was extensively altered and the water-wheel replaced by a diesel engine. In a labour intensive industry, men, women and children made linen and calico into fashionable gentlemen's starched collars. Among the styles produced were the 'Hatfield' for admirers of Lord Salisbury, the 'Roseberry' for the admirers of the sporting earl and the 'Windsor' for the royalists. A particular favourite for the devoted fan of fashion was the 'Baden Powell', a $2\frac{3}{4}$in. high jugular vein cutter popularised by the hero of the Boer War and founder of the boy scout movement.

At the end of the Great War, men's fashions changed while new technology replaced hand labour, and in 1935, the company closed down. For many years afterwards the building was used as the town's labour exchange.

Near to Vincent's factory, in Northam Causeway, McBryde & Orr operated a shirt factory until it too fell victim to progress. Despite a survival plan which laid off 160 out of its workforce of 200, the company went bankrupt in 1930.

After a short shipbuilding boom after the war, most of the Torridgeside shipyards similarly went into decline. A correspondent to the *Daily Telegraph* painted a grim description of the collapse:

> . . . down by Cleave Houses where they used to build such sturdy little fishing craft and coasting vessels, silence and desolation reign, slips are a tangle of grass and nettles . . .

Under post-war railway company amalgamation, the London and South Western Railway Co. serving Bideford became absorbed in the southern railway network. Tourists came by rail – and in increasing numbers by road – to explore and savour Charles Kingsley's 'Little White Town'.

Henry Williamson's best-selling novel, *Tarka the Otter*, published in 1927, attracted many admirers to North Devon and Bideford in particular, to search out the otter's hunting territories.

But war clouds had gathered once more over Europe. The high summer of 1939 was to be the last holiday season for five traumatic years. Luckily Bideford escaped war damage, and the closest incidents occurred when two German bombs exploded harmlessly in open country near Littleham and Instow. Mr. Battrick, manager of the *Strand* cinema, never had to fire the twin Lewis machine guns mounted on the cinema roof in order to defend nearby war factories from enemy attack.

Because they preyed on carrier pigeons carrying messages from sailors and seamen in distress on the high seas, peregrine falcons became unwitting war casualties. At Bucks Mills, Mark Braund, paying out the rope, lowered an intrepid Mrs. Berge down the shale cliffs to destroy the peregrines' nests. By the end of the war the falcon had become, and still is, an endangered species on the North Devon coast.

The Combined Operations and Experimental Establishment (C.O.X.E.) requisitioned Westward Ho! foreshore to test out inventions designed to demolish fortifications guarding the approaches to Hitler's Atlantic wall. The most bizarre of the weapons must be the 'Great Panjundrum', a cable drum packed with explosives which spat smoke and flames from its rocket propulsion units as it rumbled over the sands with the aim of detonating against enemy obstacles. But it did not work! At the end of the war, C.O.X.E. was disbanded. The Amphibious Trials and Training Unit, Royal Marines (ATTURM) now carry out equipment evaluation and training at Instow.

With the return of peace, mass car ownership sounded the death knell for thousands of miles of railway track. In 1965, the Beeching axe put an end to passenger services on the Barnstaple-Bideford-Torrington line and freight traffic ceased in 1982. Bideford's station is now a branch of Martins Bank and the goods yard is the Ethelwynne Brown Close development of old people's flats. Torrington station became the 'Puffing Billy' restaurant.

By the late 1960s, the rapid increase of road traffic had placed an intolerable strain on the Longbridge. In 1967, the Bridge Trustees were forced to spend £30,000 to repair cracks and corroded reinforcing rods in the western arches. The Trustees wrote to the then Minister of Transport, Mrs. Barbara Castle, in June 1967, expressing their grave concern for the bridge's safety, and enquiring whether the Ministry would take over full responsibility for the bridge. No reply had been received to the letter when on the night of 9 January 1968, the two western arches of the Longbridge crumbled into the river, thereby cutting Bideford in half. Main utilities carried in the bridge included the transatlantic telephone cable.[4] But there was a cost in human life to pay when the 63-year-old foreman, Tommy Mordey of Mansfield, was crushed to death by a falling crane during the repairs. However, by the end of March, a temporary roadway had been opened. The Ministry agreed to take over the bridge backdated to the time of the collapse and to pay compensation to the Bridge Trustees.

The 1961 census revealed that the population of Bideford Borough stood at 10,265. In August 1962 Bideford's planners gave permission for go-kart racing to be held at the new cattle market off Chanters Lane. Five years later, Mayor Mrs. Vivian Patt opened the Bideford Zoo at Ford House. Within a week over 1,000 people had passed through the turnstiles. But rising costs and inadequate receipts forced the Zoo into early liquidation.

At Exeter Crown Court (1973) Captain Godfrey Simmonds of Northam was acquitted of the murder of his wife. The media called the trial the 'No Body' case as the corpse of Mrs. Simmonds has never been found. The Norman Scott affair of 1979 forced the untimely resignation from public life of Jeremy Thorpe, Bideford's ex-Member of Parliament and Leader of the Liberal Party, who had been beaten by 8,473 votes in the 1979 General Election. The successful candidate was the Conservative, Tony Speller.

Fig. 25.   Honestone Street, once the main road leading out of Bideford.

Post-war slum clearance drastically altered the face of the town centre. Parts of Bridge Street, Allhalland Street, Chapel Street and Union Street (completely) disappeared. Pimlico Place, most of Providence Row and parts of Honestone were flattened. In 1972, New Street fell victim to the bulldozers. Pressure from conservationists saved Bull Hill from the wreckers, and, carefully restored, the new development is a credit to the town. Modern council housing provided accommodation for those affected by the clearances as well as workers at new factories such as A.M.P. of Great Britain Ltd., manufacturers of solderless wiring devices, at Barton Tors, East-the-Water; and Anglo-American Vulcanized Fibres on the Clovelly Road. The most original of Bideford's exporting industries is the Supreme Magic Company of 94, High Street. Private estates of easy-to-manage retirement homes became a post-war feature of Bideford and Northam.

Westward Ho! lost its genteel image when it became a centre for caravans and self-catering holidays. Although in 1962 the Devon county council planning department asked local authorities to discourage development in the Northam Burrows, Bucks Mills and Clovelly areas to preserve their environmental attractions, only the latter had virtually escaped encroachment by the 1980s. While tourism brought profit to the area, it also brought problems, particularly in regard to water supply, sewage and roads. The drought of 1976, when domestic water supplies were cut off and street standpipes introduced, underlined the South West Water Authority's inability to provide adequate services for an expanding society during crisis periods.

In the 1980s, a building embargo forbade developments in the town because of the inadequacy of the sewage disposal system which dated back to the cholera-ridden years of the Victorian age. After months of protest organised by the Torridge Action Group (T.A.G.), the Torridge district council rejected by 20 votes to 15 the plan of the South West Water Authority to build a £4.8 million fine-screen sewage plant to be sited close to the new cattle market at Bank End. With little refinement, the macerated residuum would have been debouched into the Torridge as it had been previously.

Another environmental body, the Bideford Action Group, led by Miss Sheila Hutchinson of Orchard Hill, failed in its campaign to have the new £15.3 million bridge carrying a Bideford by-pass sited to the south of the town. After an exhaustive public enquiry, the Department of the Environment decided that the 640-metre, high level bridge should follow the Department's preferred route, crossing the river at Westleigh to link up with the west bank close to the defunct Bideford Shipyard's premises.

Probably the most dramatic post-war sea rescue involving Appledore's lifeboat, *Louisa Ann Hawkins*, occurred during the late afternoon and evening of 17 November 1962 when the naval auxiliary tanker, *Green Ranger*, under tow to Cardiff for a refit, broke her towline and struck the Longpeak Reef to the west of Hartland quay. In a combined air and sea rescue, the Appledore lifeboat, coxswain Sidney Cann, managed to get alongside the stricken ship, and held position for 15 minutes trying to attract the attention of the crew. Despite the grave danger of the *Louisa* being smashed to matchwood, Cann was not to know until he had stood out to sea that the eight men aboard had been lifted to safety by the Hartland Life Saving Association team. The *Green Ranger* was a total wreck though some parts salvaged from her are preserved at the *Hartland Quay Hotel*. The Royal Lifeboat Institute awarded Coxswain Cann with their silver medal; seven crewmen, J.R. Bowden, W.G. Cann, L.G.W. Richards, T.J. Hewell, W. Evans, S. Bowden and C. Cox, were presented with the Institute's vellum certificate. The men of Hartland's L.S.A. team received the Association's coveted 'wreck service' shield.

Coxswain Sidney Cann died in March 1984. During his distinguished career with the R.N.L.I., he had been awarded the B.E.M., two R.N.L.I. bronze medals, one silver medal, three expressions of thanks on vellum and a silver medal and testimonial from the Spanish government.

A shipwreck within a few hundred yards of Hartland Point Coastguard lookout station in January 1984 recalled the bad old days of the wreckers, when over 200 men, women and children swarmed aboard the abandoned Panamanian *Joanna*, 978 tons, and carried off everything they could lay their hands on, from expensive direction-finding equipment to the crew's Christmas tree. Much of the loot was recovered and the Receiver of Wrecks did not press prosecutions. Why the *Joanna*, much troubled by labour disputes, ran up the beach has never been satisfactorily explained.

On a more pleasurable level, the last ocean-going paddle-steamer, *Waverley*, began summer day trips between Bideford, Ilfracombe and Lundy Island in 1981. The *Waverley* replaced the White Funnel Company's *Balmoral* when the company withdrew from the Bristol Channel. In 1984 the Landmark Trust, leaseholders of Lundy Island, switched the harbour base of their supply ship *Polar Bear* from Ilfracombe to Bideford.

In the post-war years, farming underwent an agrarian revolution when sophisticated machinery replaced labour and feed silos and factory-built livestock sheds dwarfed ancient shippons. Computerised milking parlours combined with intensive farming methods boosted dairy output to previously undreamt-of levels. Notwithstanding the advances made in livestock and grass husbandry, the coastline of North Devon has retained much of its centuries-old patchwork pattern of small fields.

Fig. 26 Gurnay's 800-year old Longbridge. On 29 October 1984 work began on a new river bridge and bypass to the north of Bideford.

Several Bidefordians took part in the Falkland Island conflict of 1982. Lieutenant Commander Hugh Lomas, R.N., of Cornborough, received the Distinguished Service Cross (D.S.C.). Eighteen-year-old seaman, Paul Dunn, escaped injury when an Argentine cannon shell exploded close to him wounding four of his mates. Requisitioned for war service, the fire-fighting tug *Wimpey Seahorse*, built by Appledore Shipbuilders in their enclosed yard, was praised for the part she played in the campaign. The official opening of the yard in April 1970 coincided with the launching of the 3,000-ton sand dredger, *Pen Stour*. At Watertown, Appledore, J. Hink's Watertown yard built an authentic ocean-going replica of Drake's *Golden Hind* as well as other famous exploration ships.

On 9 July 1984 Bruce Pell, spokesman for the South West Water Authority, warned that those who were caught flouting the hosepipe ban, brought in because of the summer drought, faced immediate prosecution and a fine of up to £400. The ban applied to the whole of Devon with the exception of those areas supplied by the six-year-old Wimbleball reservoir, i.e. Exeter and Tiverton. A newly-built centrally heated semi-detatched house on the Londonderry Farm Estate was on offer at that time to be sold at £26,950.

Sometime during the 1980s Gurnay's Longbridge will celebrate its 700th anniversary. Charles Kingsley, in *Westward Ho!*, describes the relationship the Bidefordian feels for his town and historic Longbridge:

> Everyone who knows Bideford cannot but know Bideford Bridge; for it is . . . the soul around which the town as a body has organised itself; and as Edinburgh is Edinburgh by virtue of its Castle, Rome, Rome by virtue of its Capitol, and Egypt, Egypt by virtue of its Pyramids, so is Bideford Bideford by virtue of its Bridge.

Appendix One

DERIVATIONS OF SOME BIDEFORD PLACE-NAMES

Allhalland Street: after Allhallows chapel
Bull Hill: centre of bull-baiting
Buttgarden Street: site of town's archery butts
Cleave Houses: houses on the cliff
Coldharbour: roadside shelter
Conduit Lane: where a drain ran from Allhalland Street into the Torridge
Cooper Street: centre of cask and barrel manufacture
Grenville Street: originally Emma Street after the wife of Richard Heard, the builder
Gunstone Street: centre of cannonball manufacture
High Street: known in the 13th century as 'Magnus Vicus', the Great Way
Honestone Street: derived from 'Horestone', an ancient boundary stone
Little America: corruption of 'Littleham Mere'
Meddon Street: corruption of 'maiden' or perhaps 'midden'
Mill Street: once the site of a water mill, later a tannery
North Street: previously 'Potter's Lane'
Nunnery Walk: lane leading to a nunnery
Pitt Lane: place where a culm mine was worked
Queen Street: previously 'Little Lane'
Rope Walk: where rope was plaited
Sentry Corner: where watchmen guarded the approaches to the town from Torrington and Barnstaple. Alternatively a corruption of 'sanctuary' or chapel

Appendix Two

THE BIDEFORD WITCHES

WITCHCRAFT became a capital crime in England in 1542. The majority of those charged with the offence were mentally disturbed old women, often physically handicapped and desperately poor. Their accusers were mostly neurotic with irrational religious obsessions. Among the unfortunates accused of witchcraft were Temperance Lloyd, Susannah Edwards and Mary Trembles, who lived together in a cottage in the Upper Gunstone Street area of Bideford Old Town.[1] Temperance Lloyd, the 'coven' leader, earned a few pence in the summer by selling apples in the town. Many parents forbade their children to buy her fruit lest the old crone put the evil eye on them. In 1679 Temperance was arrested, accused of bewitching Ann Fellows, but released because of lack of evidence. In the following year, she was found not guilty at Exeter Assizes on witchcraft charges brought against her by William Herbert of Bideford. On 26 July 1682 she was arrested on a warrant signed by Bideford's mayor, Thomas Gift, and Alderman John Davie, and charged with bewitching Dorcas Coleman, wife of John Coleman, of Bideford. In jail, Temperance incriminated her housemates Susannah Edwards and Mary Trembles, who were arrested. The three women appeared for examination before the magistrates. What follows is a synopsis of the proceedings against the three women:

The information of Dorcas Coleman, wife of John Coleman, Mariner

Dorcas Coleman stated that from August 1680 she had been stricken with pains in her arms, stomach and heart. A Thomas Bremincon called in Dr. Beare, who after examining the sick woman, diagnosed that her pains had been caused by witchcraft. Dorcas claimed that the pains were worst when the apparition of Susannah Edwards appeared in her bedchamber. These visitations had been going on for several weeks. When Dorcas confronted Susannah in jail, the accused confessed to her witchery, begging for forgiveness.

The information of Thomas Bremincon

Bremincon confirmed Dorcas Coleman's account of Dr. Beare's visit and added that after the doctor's departure, Susannah Edwards appeared in the bedchamber. Immediately

90

Dorcas's pains became so severe she could neither speak nor see, but she was able to point in Susannah's direction.

The information of Grace Thomas

Grace Thomas stated that on or about 2 February 1680 she had suffered from severe headaches and pains in all her limbs which continued until August. On 30 September, she encountered Temperance Lloyd in the High Street. Temperance fell on her knees and wept saying, 'Mistress Grace, I am glad to see you so strong'. Grace asked her, 'Why do you weep for me?'. Temperance replied, 'I weep for joy to see you so well again'.

That night, Grace became ill with pains, 'as though pins and awls had been thrust into her body from the crown of her head to the soles of her feet'. During the night of 1 June, she was stricken with pricking pains in her stomach, 'all of a sudden her belly was as two bellies'. She thought she was dying. On the Friday night, she was subjected to 'such cruel, thrusting pains in her head, shoulders, arms, hands, thighs and legs as though the flesh would have immediately torn from the bones with a man's finger and thumb'. She claimed that since Temperance's arrest, the pains had ceased. She believed that Temperance Lloyd had bewitched her.

The information of Elizabeth Eastchurch, wife of Thomas Eastchurch

Elizabeth stated that Grace Thomas, who was her lodger, had complained of pricking pains in her knee. When she examined Grace's knee, she noticed nine places which had been pricked as though by a thorn. Elizabeth approached Temperance Lloyd and demanded if she had 'any wax or clay in the form of a picture [doll] in the image of Grace Thomas which she pricked to induce pain' in her victim. Temperance denied she possessed such an object, but admitted she had a piece of leather which she had pricked nine times.

The information of Anne Wakely, wife of William Wakely, Husbandman

Anne Wakely stated that she had physically examined Temperance Lloyd in jail on the orders of the Mayor to establish if the accused had any physical abnormalities to indicate that she was a witch. In Temperance Lloyd's 'secret parts' she found 'two teats hanging nigh together, like unto a piece of flesh that a child had sucked; and that each of the said teats was about an inch long', a sure sign that she was indeed a witch. She questioned the accused as to whether she had been suckled at that place 'by the Black Man, meaning the Devil'. Temperance admitted that she had.

Witness further stated she had attended upon Grace Thomas for the previous six weeks. On one occasion she had noticed an object in the shape of a magpie flapping at Grace's bedroom window. Temperance told her that the magpie was the Black Man in the shape of a bird.

Honor Hooper, servant of Thomas Eastchurch, confirmed Anne Wakely's evidence.

The information of Temperance Lloyd

Temperance Lloyd stated that on the afternoon of 30 September 1680 she had met the Devil in the likeness of a Black Man in Higher Gunstone Lane. He persuaded her to accompany him to the home of Thomas Eastchurch in order to torment Grace Thomas. Together they entered the house, the Black Man now in the form of a braget [grey] cat. There they found Anne Wakely massaging Grace Thomas's arms. Invisible to the two women, Temperance pinched Grace's arms, shoulders, thighs and legs. Later, in the street, Temperance saw the braget cat enter Thomas Eastchurch's shop. On the following day she entered Thomas Eastchurch's shop with the Black Man, again disguised as a braget cat. Although persons were present in the house, she and the cat were invisible to them. On another occasion, she and the Black Man entered Grace's bedchamber and found Grace in a 'very sad condition'. Notwithstanding her condition, the Black Man proceeded to torment her 'on purpose to put the said Grace out of her life'.

She admitted she had knelt down in the street to enable the Black Man to suck her secret teats. She estimated the Black Man's height to be about the length of her arm and that his eyes were very big. In the street he kept hopping or leaping before her, 'and afterwards did suck her as she was lying down'. On 1 June, she and the Black Man tormented Grace Thomas for more than two hours with the intention of killing her. Although Anne Wakely was in the room, Temperance and the Black Man remained invisible to her.

On the completion of her statement, the accused was questioned on her previous indictments for witchcraft. The Major and Justices agreed that the accused had a case to answer. But because 'they were dissatisfied in some particulars concerning the piece of leather . . . that there might be some enchantment used in or about the leather', the women were sent to the parish church for interrogation by the vicar, Mr. Ogilby, a cleric given to hard drinking and bouts of violence.

Ogilby elicited that Temperance had appeared to Lydia Burman, deceased, in the form of a red pig, when she was 'brewing in the house of Humphrey Ackland of Biddiford'. Temperance refused to answer some of Ogilby's questions 'for if he discovered the same, the Devil would tear her to pieces'. She added further details of the appearance of the little Black Man, saying he 'wore blackish clothes, had broad eyes, and had a mouth like a toad'.

William Edwards swore that he had heard Susannah Edwards claim that the Devil had carnal knowledge of her body. Thomas Jones stated that Susannah had told a certain John Dunning that she had met the Black Man in Parsonage Close. Later, she and Mary Trembles tortured Grace Barnes and Dorcas Coleman by witchcraft. Mary said that the Devil had appeared to her in the shape of a lion. Susannah also recounted how the Devil in the guise of a boy lay with her in bed, and that 'it was very cold for her'. On another occasion she had met the 'boy' in Stambridge Lane, off the Abbotsham Road.

Joanna Jones gave evidence that her husband had been bewitched by Susannah Edwards. Mr. Jones had 'capered like a mad-man, and fell a-shaking, quivering and foaming, and lay for a space of half an hour like a deadman'.

Ogilby required Temperance to recite the Lord's Prayer which she failed to do to his satisfaction, a further indication she was indeed a witch. The magistrates committed the three women for trial at Exeter.

At Exeter Assizes on 18 August, Temperance, Susannah and Mary were found guilty of witchcraft. Judge Raymond condemned the three to be hanged. A week later, the condemned women were brought to the gallows at Heavitree outside the city limits.

Temperance 'went all the way eating and was seemingly unconcerned', Susannah also went quietly enough, but Mary Trembles 'was very loath to be hanged, and in order to get her to the gallows, she was strapped to a horse'.

Lined up beneath the gallows crossbar, the hangman slipped the nooses about their necks. A local minister, the Reverend Hann, subjected the women to further questioning before their execution. He began with the distraught Mary Trembles:

Hann: What have you to say as to the crime you are now to die for?

Mary: I have spoken as much as I can speak already, and can speak no more.

Hann: In what shape did the Devil come to you?

Mary: The Devil came to me once, I think, like a lion.

Hann: Did he offer violence to you?

Mary: No, not at all. He frightened me, but he did nothing to me. And I cried out to God, and asked what he would have, and the Devil vanished.

Hann: Did he give you gifts, or make you a promise?

Mary: No.

Hann: Had he any of your blood?

Mary: No.

Hann: Did he come to make use of your body?

Mary: Never in my life.

Hann: Have you a secret teat?

Mary: No.

Hann: Mary Trembles, was not the Devil there with Susannah when I was once in prison with you; and under your coats: the others told me he was there but is now fled: and that the Devil was in the way when I was going to Taunton with my son, who is a Minister? You speak as a dying woman, and as the Psalm says: 'I will confess my iniquities and acknowledge all my sins . . .'. If you break your compact with the Devil and make a covenant with God you may also obtain mercy. If you have anything to say, speak your mind.

Mary: I have spoken the truth, and can say no more; Mr. Hann, I would desire Temperance and Susannah come by me and confess as I have done.

Hann turned his attention to Temperance Lloyd:

Hann: Temperance Lloyd, have you made any contract with the Devil?

Temp: No.

Hann: Did he ever take any of your blood?

Temp: No.

Hann: How did he appear to you at the first, or where, in the street? In what shape?

Temp: In a woeful shape.

Hann: Had he ever any carnal knowledge of you?

Temp: No, never.

Hann: What did he do when he came to you?

Temp: He caused me to go and do harm.

Hann: And did you go?

Temp: I hurt a woman against my conscience: he carried me to her door which was open. The woman's name was Grace Thomas.

Hann: What made you harm her? Did she ever do you any harm?

Temp: No, she never did me any harm: but the Devil beat me about the head grievously because I would not kill her, but I did bruise her after my fashion.

Hann: Did you bruise her until the blood gushed out of her mouth and nose?

Temp: No.

Hann: How many did you destroy and hurt?

Temp: None but she.

Hann: Did you know any mariners that you, or your associates destroyed by overturning their ships and boats?

Temp: No, I never hurt any ship, barque, or boat in my life.

Hann: Was it you, or Satan, that did bewitch the children?

Temp: I sold apples. A child took an apple from me, and the mother took the apple from the child, for which I was very angry: but the child died from smallpox.

Hann: Did you know one Mr. Luttrell of these parts, or any of your confederates? Did you bewitch his child?

Temp: No.

Hann: Temperance, how did you come to hurt Mrs. Grace Thomas? Did you pass through the keyhole, or was the door open?

Temp: The Devil led me up the stairs, and the door was open: and this is all the hurt I did.

Hann: How did you know it was the Devil?

Temp: I knew it by his eyes.

Hann: Had you no discourse or compact with him?

Temp: No: he said I should go with him to destroy a woman, and I told him I would not. He said he would make me, and then the Devil beat me about the head.

Hann: Why had you not called upon God?

Temp: He would not let me do it.

Hann: You say you never hurt ships nor boats: did you never ride over the sea on a cow?

Temp: No, no. It was she – [Susannah Edwards].

Hann then questioned Susannah Edwards.

Hann: Susan, did you see the shape of a bullock? At the first time of your examination you said it was a short black man, about the length of your arm?

Susan: He was black, sir.

Hann: Had you any knowledge of the bewitching of Mr. Luttrell's child, or did you know a place called Tranton-Burroughs?

Susan: No.

Hann: Are you willing to have prayers?

Mr. Hann prayed but the three women did not join him. At the wish of Susannah, the three recited part of the 40th Psalm, 'I waited patiently for the Lord: and he inclined unto me, and heard my cry . . .' In the last seconds of her life, Susannah prayed aloud: 'Lord Jesus speed me; though my sins be as red as scarlet, thou Lord Jesus can make them as white as snow: the Lord help my soul.' The hangman turned her into space. Mary Trembles was the next to go. Temperance Lloyd's ordeal was not yet over. The Sheriff put a series of questions to her:

Sher: You are looked on as the woman that has debauched the other two. Did you ever lie with the Devil?

Temp: No.

Sher: Did you know of his coming to jail?

Temp: No.

Sher: Have you anything to say to satisfy the world?

Temp: I forgive them, as I desire the Lord Jesus Christ to forgive me. The greatest thing I did was to Mrs. Grace Thomas and I desire I may be forgiven for it; and that the Lord Jesus Christ may forgive me. The Devil met me in the street and bid me kill her: and because I would not, he beat me about the head and back.

Sher: In what shape or colour was he?

Temp: In black, like a bullock.

Sher: How did you know you did it? How went you in, through the keyhole or the door?

Temp: By the door.

Sher: Had you discourse with the Devil?

Temp: Never but this day six weeks ago.

Sher: You were charged about 12 years ago, and did you never see the Devil but this time?

Temp: Yes, once before. I was going for furze, and he came to me and said, 'This poor woman has a great burden', and he would help me carry my burden, and I said, 'The Lord has enabled me to carry it so far, and I hope I shall be able to carry it further'.

Sher: Did the Devil never promise you anything?

Temp: No, never.

Sher: Then you have served a very bad master who gave you nothing. Well consider you are just departing this world, do you believe there is a God?

Temp: Yes.
Sher: Do you believe in Jesus Christ?
Temp: Yes, and I pray Jesus Christ to pardon all my sins.

The hangman pushed away the trestle and Temperance joined Mary and Susannah, dancing a grisly jig of death.

Later Mary Beare and Elizabeth Cadely, contemporaries of the Bideford witches, appeared before Bideford magistrates to answer accusations of witchcraft. Both were discharged. In 1686, several complaints of witchery were made against Abigail, wife of Robert Handford. These charges were also dropped.

As a footnote to the tragedy of the Bideford witches, a mariner claimed he had met the three women in Parsonage Close. He had seen a 'little Black man' come out of the rectory. The creature had a spiked tail and cloven feet. He took an object out of a pouch and gave it to the three women who put it in a crock. The little man then vanished. The mariner heard Susannah Edwards croak: 'Thrice the brindled cat hath mewed'. The women greeted the words with peals of laughter. Then the women chanted a ditty which Bideford children sang for years afterwards:

Beat the water Tremble's daughter
Till the tempest gather o'er us;
Till the thunder strike with wonder,
And the lightning flash before us;
Beat the water, Tremble's daughter,
Rain seize our foes and slaughter.

Was there another unfortunate Bideford woman executed for witchcraft? In *Notes and Queries* appearing in the Devon Association, 18 June 1932, there appears the following query:

The Undutiful Daughter: Who was she? She lived at Bideford, bore a child to a Mr. Lawrence of that place, and was finally hanged for murder, after a confession of witchcraft etc. An account of her in a chapbook printed in Philadelphia, 1765, is before me, but the part of the titlepage with her name is torn off, and no other copy of the issues is known, while the lack of it makes a search for other editions a difficult matter. Her witchcraft was found by the learned Dr. H...y. Who was he? The verse text gives no help!

T.O.M.

The Witchcraft Acts were erased from the Statute Book in 1716.

NOTES

Chapter One

1. Shebbear: (O.E.) A wood from which spear shafts can be obtained.
2. Skern: From Norse 'Skaerm', meaning shelter.
3. Lundy: Norse for puffin.
4. From the Phillimore translations of Domesday Book.
5. The family spelling, 'Grenvile', will be used in narrative.
6. Local tradition claims that the siting of the bridge came to Gurnay in a vision. Another legend suggests that Gurnay laid the bridge's foundation stones at the ford to the south of the town, only to find them swept by the tide to the place where the present bridge stands.
7. Now on view at Portsmouth.
8. Five miles (7km.) west of Bideford.

Chapter Two

1. Possibly the *Santa Maria*. See page 20.
2. At Appledore Maritime Museum. Reputed to have come from the *San Juan*.

Chapter Three

1. Tuly Street, Barnstaple.
2. On the A30 between Okehampton and Launceston.
3. The battle site can be identified by the *Stamford Hotel* off the A39 on the eastern outskirts of Bude.
4. Now on the front wall of *Tree Inn*, Stratton, Sir Bevil's headquarters.
5. The rat flea, *Xenopsylla Cheopsis*, can survive away from its host for up to six months.

Chapter Four

1. Now North Road.
2. Identified by Tweenaways Stores, former tollhouse, Clovelly Road.
3. Supposed to be the longest continuously occupied site in England.
4. Sober coloured.

5.   Site of Masonic Hall.
6.   Now Abbotsham Court.
7.   Since removed. Possibly inset in wall at junction of the quay and High Street (see plate 33).

Chapter Five

1.   Forerunners of the modern police force.
2.   Gen. Edward Pine Coffin of Alwington served with distinction as a Commissary in Ireland during the Great Hunger, 1845-9. In recognition of his work in famine relief, he received a knighthood. He served with equal dedication in alleviating hardship in the notorious Highland Clearances in the 1850s.
3.   The first dissenting chapel to be licensed was 'Little Meeting' in 1694. In 1753 Rev. Samuel Lavington was inducted into 'Great Meeting' in Bridgeland Street now named after Lavington.
4.   Kingsley is supposed to have written part of the novel in the *Royal Hotel*, East-the-Water.
5.   Thomas Chanter built a 'folly' tower in the grounds of his Appledore home to enable him to watch his ships crossing the harbour bar. Demolished 1952.

Chapter Six

1.   Seapies: Oyster catchers.
2.   A Molesworth family name dating back to the reign of Dutch-born William III, Prince of Nassau (1688-1702) when the monarch stood as godfather to the 1st Viscount Molesworth.
3.   The town's gas works opened in 1853 on the site of the former French P.O.W. camp, East-the-Water.
4.   Closed January 1981 after 150 years.

INDEX

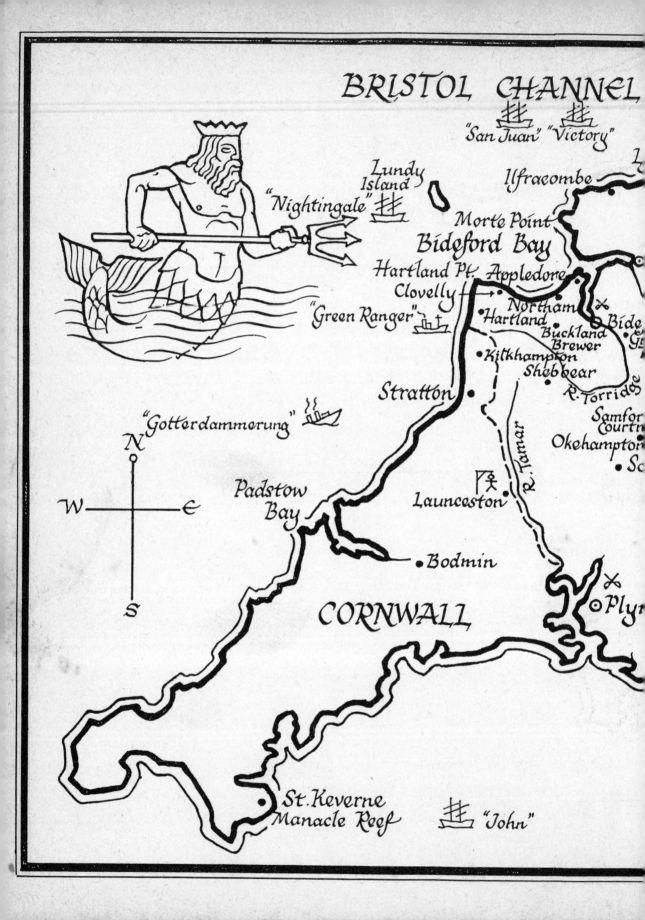

BRISTOL CHANNEL

"San Juan" "Victory"

Lundy Island   Ilfracombe

"Nightingale"   Morte Point

Bideford Bay

Hartland Pt.   Appledore

Clovelly   Northam   Bide

Hartland   Buckland   G

"Green Ranger"   Brewer

Kilkhampton   Shebbear

Stratton   R. Torridge

Samfor
Courtn

Okehampton

Sc

"Gotterdammerung"

N

Launceston

W   E

Padstow
Bay

S

Bodmin

CORNWALL

Plyr

St. Keverne
Manacle Reef   "John"